PRAISE FOR *MY ANXIOUS MIND*

My Anxious Mind is a terrific book! It contains easy-to-understand information and practical, straightforward steps anyone can take to reduce undue anxiety. It's a must read for anxious teens and their parents and teachers but will be helpful to individuals of any age who have an "anxious mind."

Judith S. Beck, PhD
Director, Beck Institute for Cognitive Therapy and Research
Clinical Associate Professor of Psychology in Psychiatry,
University of Pennsylvania
Past President, Academy of Cognitive Therapy

This wonderful book is a must buy for adolescents and their families with severe anxiety. Its two voices—the recently affected adolescent and the experienced clinician—offer invaluable insights into the potentially devastating effects of untreated anxiety while describing in detail proven strategies for taking charge of fears and obsessions.

Glen R. Elliott, PhD, MD
Chief Psychiatrist and Medical Director,
The Children's Health Council, Palo Alto, CA
Author of *Medicating Young Minds: How to Know If Psychiatric
Drugs Will Help or Hurt Your Child*

The strategies discussed in *My Anxious Mind* are firmly grounded in the latest research on treating anxiety. At the same time, the book is highly accessible, engaging, and easy to follow. I highly recommend *My Anxious Mind* to any teen who struggles with high levels of anxiety. Their parents should read it, too!

Martin M. Antony, PhD, ABPP
Professor of Psychology, Ryerson University, Toronto
Author of *The Anti-Anxiety Workbook*

Up to one in five teens suffer from a significant anxiety disorder while countless others experience milder fears and worries. Tompkins and Martinez offer a step-by-step guide to anxiety management written specifically for adolescents. Along with proven techniques for dealing with anxious thoughts, physical symptoms of anxiety, and avoidance behaviors, this valuable book also addresses the important areas of sleep, nutrition, and exercise.

John Piacentini, PhD, ABPP
Professor of Psychiatry and Biobehavioral Sciences,
UCLA David Geffen School of Medicine
Director, Child OCD, Anxiety, and Tic Disorders Program,
Semel Institute for Neuroscience and Human Behavior, UCLA

My Anxious Mind: A Teen's Guide to Managing Anxiety and Panic, is a marvelous book for teens who feel anxious or shy sometimes or find that anxiety or shyness is becoming too frequent and too painful. If anxiety is interfering with teens making friends, doing what they want to, asserting themselves, or asking for help, this is the book for them. Tompkins and Martinez have written this guide with precision and clarity, while communicating warmth to their young readers and a real understanding of the challenges of the teen-age years. How great it will be to have a personal guide for handling adolescent worries and thoughts about what look like impending social disasters; and for solving the inevitable interpersonal problems and challenges of dealing with those teens love, like, can't stand, and learn to like. Teens can all learn from these authors' experience and wisdom.

Lynne Henderson, PhD
Director, The Shyness Institute, Palo Alto, California
Author of *The Social Fitness Training Manuals*

My Anxious Mind

A Teen's Guide to Managing Anxiety and Panic

MY ANXIOUS MIND

A TEEN'S GUIDE to MANAGING ANXIETY and PANIC

by Michael A. Tompkins, PhD and Katherine A. Martinez, PsyD

illustrated by Michael Sloan

Magination Press • American Psychological Association • Washington, DC

For Madeleine and Olivia; not teens yet, but on the cusp — MAT

For Jack, who teaches me every day — KAM

Published by
MAGINATION PRESS
An Educational Publishing Foundation Book
American Psychological Association
750 First Street, NE
Washington, DC 20002

For more information about our books, including a complete catalog, please write to us, call 1-800-374-2721, or visit our website at www.maginationpress.com.

Typeset in Sabon by Circle Graphics, Columbia, MD
Printed by Sheridan Books, Ann Arbor, MI

Library of Congress Cataloging-in-Publication Data
Tompkins, Michael A.
  My anxious mind : a teen's guide to managing anxiety and panic / by Michael A. Tompkins and Katherine A. Martinez ; illustrated by Michael Sloan.
    p. cm.
  ISBN-13: 978-1-4338-0450-2 (pbk. : alk. paper)
  ISBN-10: 1-4338-0450-6 (pbk. : alk. paper)   1. Anxiety in adolescence—Popular works. 2. Panic—Popular works. I. Martinez, Katherine A. II. Title.
  RJ506.A58T66 2009
  618.92'8522—dc22
                                    2009011442
10 9 8 7 6

CONTENTS

Contents

NOTE TO READER

Think about how your life would be different if you were less anxious. What would change in your life? Would you try new activities or make new friends? Would you sleep better and have more free time because you study less?

Whether you are reading *My Anxious Mind* on your own, in a group, or with a parent, counselor, or psychotherapist, the tools and strategies described here may help you manage your worry and fear. We have helped many teens calm their anxious minds by creating individualized plans based on these tools. These tools are similar to those you might learn in cognitive–behavior therapy (CBT), a type of psychotherapy that teaches you to restore the ability of your mind and body to calm itself. We know CBT tools work, and we think they can work for you, too. We invite you to begin by completing the exercises and practicing the tools. You can work this practice into your daily routine. So, can you spare 30 minutes to feel less anxious?

Before you get started, we would like to offer some advice up front. We understand that no two teens are the same and that some things you read in this book may fit for you and other things may not. That is okay. We only ask that you use the tools and strategies that are helpful for your situation. And like so many things, success depends more on what you do than on what you want to do. Staying motivated to make a change will take some effort. Knowing that, we would like to encourage you to

- Take charge of your plan,
- Promise to keep going,
- Take small risks, and
- Admit the benefits of fear and worry and give them back!

TAKE CHARGE OF YOUR PLAN

If your teachers did not load you with so much homework or if your friends or family didn't stress you out so much, would you be less anxious? Maybe, but you can control how much these things affect you. You are in charge of your anxious mind, not anyone else—not your parents, teachers, or friends. This may be tough for you to accept. However, taking charge is probably the most important and empowering step you can take. Taking charge means you do not blame your friends, your school, your parents, or yourself. Taking charge means taking back control. Taking charge also means leading the charge, not doing it all alone.

PROMISE TO KEEP GOING

Learning to calm your anxious mind will take time and practice. Even if you are very motivated to become less anxious, you will find that some days your anxiety is back. That is okay. On other days, you might not feel like doing anything. That is okay, too. It is hard to keep going after you have had a tough day and you wonder whether you will ever feel less anxious. But that cannot be a reason to stop practicing. Instead, try to promise yourself that you will work on your plan for at least three months and see what happens. And from time to time, take a look back. You will see that you are ahead of where you began. You are getting there, and that is progress that will help you to keep going.

TAKE SMALL RISKS

To live your life fully is to take risks—small ones and big ones. As odd as it may sound, there is no way to calm your anxious mind without taking a chance, without risking to think and act a bit differently. If you have a phobia, that may mean facing your fear. If you have a panic attack, that might mean letting go rather than fighting against it. If your friends cause you stress, that may mean telling them how you feel. You won't need to take on all your fear at once, but if you tackle it in small steps, you can begin to break your fear and worries down, piece by piece, and learn to face them completely.

ADMIT THE BENEFITS OF FEAR AND WORRY AND GIVE THEM BACK

Have you ever told your parents that you were too stressed to do your homework or chores, when really you just did not want to do it right then? Many anxious teens have discovered some payoffs of staying anxious, but we know this does not mean you do not want to overcome your worry and fear. It just means that you have two minds when it comes to your anxiety and fear. There is your anxious mind, of course, but then, there is the other mind that is comfortable with the way things are. If you think you have some payoffs, we suggest you give them back, at least for a while, to see what you can accomplish. Otherwise, you may never know what you can do, what you can be, and how much you can succeed. We think you will see that it is totally worth it in the end.

At any time, if taking on your anxiety alone seems too tough, ask your parents or a close friend to coach you through the book.

Sometimes all it takes is a little reminder or a word of encouragement to get the ball rolling and keep it rolling. Coaches can gently nudge you toward trying hard things, while being patient and supportive along the way. It is not easy to overcome anxiety or phobias, and a good coach can really help.

However, sometimes the best coach may be a psychotherapist who has experience working with anxious teens. This is particularly true if you have extreme or intense anxiety. A professional can really help you move things along if you become stuck. If you are not in psychotherapy but would like to try it, speak to your parents. Later in this book, we will describe how you might go about asking for this kind of help if you want it.

Good luck!

Michael Tompkins and Katherine Martinez

My Anxious Mind

A Teen's Guide
to
Managing
Anxiety and Panic

CHAPTER 1

WHEN ANXIETY IS A PROBLEM

If you have an anxious mind, we want you to know—you are not alone. Did you know that about one out of every 20 teens in the United States has extreme worry, phobias, or panic attacks? It is true. Count all the kids in your grade or your school and divide this number by 20. That is a lot of teens. That is a lot of anxious minds.

If you have an anxious mind, we bet you wish that you could push a button and turn off your worry or turn a volume knob to quiet down your fears a bit. When you have an anxious mind, it feels like there is nothing that you can do. It feels like your anxious mind is in charge, not you. If you are reading this book, we bet you would like to change that. The first step to taking charge of your anxious mind is to learn as much about anxiety as you can and to become an expert. In this chapter, you will learn when anxiety is helpful and not so helpful, and we will describe three things that keep your Worry Wheel spinning. Lastly, you will hear from teens who will describe how their anxiety problems troubled them and how their anxious minds made their lives difficult.

WHAT IS ANXIETY?

Everyone feels anxious from time to time. Anxiety is a normal emotion that everyone experiences. It makes sense to be a little nervous before a major test, a first date, or before you run onto the field to play a big game. In fact, a little anxiety is a good thing—it is there to protect you. If you were walking home from school and a big dog came up to you and began to snarl at you with bared teeth, would you reach out to pet him? Probably not. That is because your anxious mind said, "Danger," and your body listened. In fact, you might slowly back away from the dog and take another path home just to be safe. At times, however, your anxious mind says that an object or situation is dangerous even when it is not or at least when the danger is very small or is unlikely. Your anxious body sometimes does not know the difference. It listens to your anxious mind and acts as if the danger is real. Your anxious body takes over to protect you, just in case, and this can lead to unhelpful anxiety.

SPINNING THE WORRY WHEEL

When you experience unhelpful anxiety, your anxious mind goes around and around like a wheel. We call this the *Worry Wheel.*

Your Worry Wheel has three parts—anxious mind, anxious body, and anxious actions. Your anxious mind includes the thoughts you have that make you anxious like, "What if I fail my math test?" or "What if she thinks I'm weird?" When your mind is anxious, you worry that something bad will happen. You worry about dropping an important pass in a football game or not sounding smart enough or cool enough to your friends. Your anxious mind certainly gets your Worry Wheel spinning. However, there is another piece that keeps your Worry Wheel spinning and that is your anxious body.

The Worry Wheel

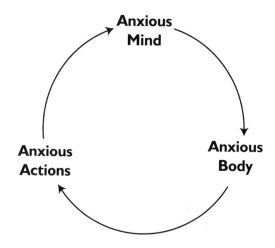

When your body is anxious, you experience a variety of physical sensations—your heart beats a bit faster, your breathing increases, you sweat, and you may feel queasy and tense. Soon, your anxious mind is feeding your anxious body and you are going around and around, faster and faster, having more thoughts that are anxious and more intense physical sensations. Your Worry Wheel is really spinning now.

After a while, your anxious actions hop aboard. Anxious actions are the things you do to play it safe or cope with your anxious mind and anxious body. It is your way to prevent something bad from happening. If you are anxious in social settings and around other people, playing it safe might mean that when another teen asks you whether you liked a certain video game, you ask what he thought about it rather than sharing your opinion. You may study for a test several hours longer than your smartest friends, just to be sure that you do well. You may stay home and avoid going out with your friends on a Friday night—all because you are anxious.

Anxious actions do not solve the problem. They just keep the Worry Wheel spinning. Sometimes, your Worry Wheel may spin so fast and so intensely that you have to leave the situation, like leaving a party or walking away from a group of kids. That might calm your anxious mind some and make your body feel less tense, but it does not really help you overcome the anxiety that keeps your Worry Wheel spinning. Those actions just put it on slow spin until the next thing sets it spinning again.

For some teens, the Worry Wheel spins often enough that their anxiety becomes intense and excessive. When thinking about your own anxiety level, defining *excessive* can be tricky, but it might help to pay attention to the four Ds:

- Is your anxiety *disproportionate* to the situation? For example, although it makes sense to feel quite anxious if a tarantula drops down in front of you, does it make sense to feel the same degree of anxiety if a daddy longlegs crosses your path? It makes sense to feel anxious about an exam on a topic that is difficult for you and for which you have not studied. Does it make sense to feel the same level of anxiety about an exam on a topic that comes easy to you and for which you and your friends have studied for many hours? If you notice that often you feel extremely anxious about things about which most other teens are only mildly worried, your anxiety might be excessive.
- Is your anxiety *disrupting* or interfering with your life? If you want more friends but your anxiety prevents you from calling other teens or going to school events, your anxiety may be excessive. If your anxiety builds during a test

such that you cannot concentrate on the questions or think clearly, even though you have studied the material, your anxiety may be excessive. Normal anxiety is there to protect you and help you function effectively in life. If your anxiety is interfering with your life and making it difficult for you to keep up with other teens your age, your anxiety may be excessive.

- Is your anxiety *distressing* to you? At times, teens with a very anxious mind get by. They ride elevators. They study and take their exams. They speak when called on in class. However, they are very anxious and uncomfortable when they do these things. If this is your situation, your anxiety might be excessive not because it disrupts your life, but because the intensity of the anxiety bothers you and bothers you a great deal.

- What is the *duration* of your anxiety? How long have you been feeling anxious? Is your anxiety an ongoing problem? If you have been anxious on and off for a long time, your anxiety may be excessive. Most anxious episodes come and go. If you are riding an elevator one day and it stops briefly between floors, you might feel a little anxious when you step on the elevator the next day. However, your anxiety will soon pass, and you will likely forget about what happened in a day or two. If your anxiety is excessive, however, you might feel anxious about riding an elevator from now on. Generally, most anxiety and fears diminish or disappear in less than six months. If your anxiety has lingered longer than that, your anxiety may be excessive.

We know that anxiety is silent and sneaky. It can exist for a long time before you realize it is getting in the way, even excessive anxiety. Here is a list of some typical areas that anxiety interferes in the lives of teens. Look them over. Is your anxious mind making any of these areas difficult for you?

- Schoolwork—Do you have trouble getting your homework in on time or settling down to get it done because you worry too much? Do you worry too much about what the teachers or other kids will think about your work? Do you get very anxious during tests or when given big school projects?
- Friendships and dating—Do you avoid saying hello to other teens because you are too anxious? Do you have trouble saying "No" because you are worried what your friends or other teens will think of you? Would you like to date but are too anxious to ask out someone?
- Family life—Do you have to ask your parents to reassure you that things will work out okay? Do you spend more time with your family than you would like just because you are too anxious to hang out with your friends? Do you and your parents often argue because they insist you push through your fears to try new things?
- Sports—Have you dropped out of sports because you are too worried about how you will do? Do you hold back because you are afraid you will make a mistake when kicking or hitting the ball? Do you become so anxious during performances or competitions that you sweat or throw up?
- Job—Are you working at a job that is boring because you are too anxious to look for another one? Do you spend too much time checking and re-checking everything you do because you are worried you will make a mistake?
- Health—Are you having trouble sleeping or not getting enough sleep? Do you skip meals or eat way too much? Do you find yourself self-medicating? In other words, do you drink

alcohol, use drugs, or engage in risky sexual behaviors because you feel anxious?

If you answered "Yes" to the four Ds in any of these areas, your anxiety is probably excessive and getting in the way. When anxiety builds to this level, it may mean you have an *anxiety disorder*. Anxiety disorders are different from normal, everyday anxiety and fearfulness in that the anxiety is more intense, lasts longer (lingers for months after the stressful situation has passed), and leads to extreme fears that can hold you back.

DESCRIBING EXCESSIVE ANXIETY

Describing your own anxiety as excessive is probably a little frightening. And thinking that you might have a problem or an anxiety disorder probably sounds scary, too. But having an anxiety disorder is not a sign that you are weak or weird. An anxiety disorder does not mean that something is seriously wrong with you. An anxiety disorder means that the same emotional response that is there to protect you is not working the way it should in certain situations.

We believe having a name for a problem is the first step in getting the right kind of help. In the next section, we will name and describe some common anxiety disorders, as well as introduce some teens who you will hear from throughout the book. If, after reading through the following information you want to learn more about a particular anxiety disorder, speak to your parents, physician, or school counselor. They may be able to answer your questions or direct you to other information that can help you get started in getting all the help you need. However, deciding whether you (or anyone) have an anxiety disorder is a complicated process, one that is best left to an experienced mental health professional.

Social Anxiety Disorder (Social Phobia)

Social anxiety disorder (or *social phobia*) is one of the most common anxiety disorders for teens. Social anxiety is an extreme and persistent fear of social or performance situations (like playing in a sporting event, playing at a recital, or taking big tests) in which embarrassment may occur or there is a risk of others negatively evaluating you. All teens experience anxiety about social situations on occasion and do not like others evaluating them in negative ways, but for some teens, social anxiety causes significant distress and prevents participation in everyday activities. Teens that have social anxiety may worry excessively about what people think or about doing or saying something embarrassing or humiliating. They may feel that any mistake will lead to a disaster, causing their teachers to yell at them or their friends to not want to hang out with them ever again.

Social anxiety can be specific or generalized. Specific social anxiety means that a person has a single social fear. The most common specific social anxiety is fear of speaking in public. That is when a teen becomes extremely anxious when she has to give a presentation to her class, or when the teacher calls on her to answer a question in class. Other common specific social anxieties include fear of using public toilets, taking tests, blushing in public, or choking on or spilling food while eating in public. The generalized type of social anxiety is less specific and involves fearing any social or group situation where you feel others might be watching or negatively evaluating you. Look at Bobbie's story.

I've been shy all my life, but it really got bad when I started mid-dle school. The school was big and the few friends I had were hanging out with new kids. I was too worried that the new kids would think I was a jerk or weird. The only conversations I had with kids were online. I made my own webpage and started my own blog, but after a while, I stopped blogging because I worried about what the kids might think about me when they read my blog. I thought my life was too boring and dumb anyway and other kids would think I was a loser. I spent most of my first year either helping my computer teacher or reading in the library. I began to hate school and sometimes pretended I was sick so I wouldn't have to go to school. Now, I'm seeing a therapist who tells me I have social anxiety disorder. I've been working on it, and I can tell you that I'm feeling less worried about what other kids think. I want them to like me, but I've learned that it's not the end of the world either if they don't.—Bobbie, age 15

Generalized Anxiety Disorder

Generalized anxiety disorder (GAD) is excessive anxiety and worry about a range of events and activities that occurs most days and is hard to turn off. It is like an anxious mind in hyper-drive. Teens with GAD pretty much worry about the same things other teens worry about (school performance, friendships, world events), except that their worry is more intense and more extreme than it is in other teens. In addition, teens with GAD feel tense or "keyed up" most days, can feel irritable, and might even have trouble sleeping. Read about Clay and GAD in the next story.

Once I start worrying, I can't seem to turn the worry down. My doctor called my kind of worry generalized anxiety disorder. We joke and call it GAD, as in gadfly, because it's always stirring things up in my mind. That's what a gadfly does—stirs things up just to stir things up. It's annoying. Because worry had been in my life for as long as I could remember, it was hard to answer the question, "When did it all start?" What I do know is that it started to bother me in sixth grade. School suddenly got much harder with the heavier workload and all. I started to worry about whether I would get into a good college, and I worried a lot. My teachers told me that I shouldn't worry so much. My grades were good, and I was a hard worker. But I still worried. Many nights I was up late checking my homework for mistakes again and again. Most nights, I couldn't fall asleep because my anxious mind was in high gear, worrying about all the things I had to do. Sometimes it would take me over an hour to fall asleep. I never thought my worry was too much until I realized that I was afraid to try out for the high school basketball team because I was too worried about messing up. That did it for me. I love basketball, and I wasn't going to let my anxious mind get in the way of me doing something I love.—Clay, age 17

Obsessive–Compulsive Disorder

Obsessive–compulsive disorder (OCD) is another kind of anxiety disorder. OCD includes extreme or unreasonable obsessions, compulsions, or both that are time consuming and cause significant distress or otherwise interfere with a person's daily functioning. Obsessions are thoughts, ideas, images, or impulses that pop into a person's mind and often cause him to feel anxious or uncomfortable. A person with OCD recognizes that these thoughts and ideas do not make any sense and tries not to think about them, but they continue to pop up for hours, days, weeks, or months. Because of the relentless way these obsessions keep popping up, teens with

OCD find themselves compulsively doing things to get rid of the thought or to prevent the bad thing from happening. A teen with OCD can spend many hours cleaning and tidying her room. Another teen might check his backpack 15 or 20 times before he can leave for school. He might also need to check that his letters are perfectly shaped and sit exactly on the lines on the page, which involve a lot of erasing and re-writing. Teens with OCD can spend many hours doing these kind of things and desperately want to stop but cannot. See how OCD started bugging Min in tenth grade. Before she knew it, this hyper-hygiene bully trapped her.

I love volleyball but stopped playing last year because I was too worried I would get sick. I didn't like the idea of touching the ball after the other kids touched it. I know this sounds strange, but I worried that I'd catch some terrible disease. I can't even tell you what disease! I've always been a bit of a germ-o-phobe. My mother's a nurse and, at first, I thought I worried about getting sick so much because of her. She was always telling me to wash my hands or to cover my mouth when I coughed or sneezed. Now I know it wasn't just my mom. I have obsessive–compulsive disorder. Before I got some help for my OCD, I took four or five showers a day. My friends asked me why my hands were always so red and chapped and wondered why I didn't want to hang out with them anymore at lunch. They didn't know I was terrified of getting sick. It wouldn't have made sense to them. I know that, because it didn't make a whole lot of sense to me either.—Min, age 16

Panic Disorder and Agoraphobia

Panic disorder includes recurrent and unexpected panic attacks. Panic attacks are very intense physical sensations such as shortness of breath, choking, sweating, chest pain, and heart palpitations, and intense feelings that make you think you are going crazy or losing control. Teens with panic disorder feel these scary sensations and worry over and over about having another panic attack. Many times, a first panic attack sets in motion a wave of more panic attacks—three or more attacks a week—until the teen seeks help.

Most teens with panic disorder begin to avoid certain situations because they believe they may not be able to escape quickly if they have a panic attack or help may be unavailable if they need it. We call this pattern of avoiding certain places or situations *agoraphobia,* which most teens with panic disorder experience to some degree. Typical places or situations that teens avoid are crowded places (shopping malls, movie theaters), enclosed spaces (tunnels, subways, planes), public transportation (trains, buses, planes), or being at home alone or far away from home without a friend or family member. Look at Darcy's story. She went from having a busy and fun life in high school to becoming a total hermit.

My therapist told me that panic disorder is fear of fear and that just about covers it. When I had my first panic attack, I thought I was going to suffocate and die. I really did. My doctor said I was fine and that I just had a panic attack, but I still worried. I really felt like I was going to die and, if I didn't die, I was sure I was going to flip out and do something embarrassing, like screaming or running around. At first, I tried to tough it out—you know, try to control myself. But I learned that the more I tried to control my anxiety, the more anxious I became. I knew I needed some help when I started passing up going out with my friends because I was worried I'd have a panic attack. I didn't want to go visit colleges because I was worried I'd have a panic attack and couldn't get back home. However, the thing that really told me

I needed help was when I was thinking about not even going to veterinary school because I was afraid. That did it. I knew I needed some help.—Darcy, age 17

Specific Phobia

A specific phobia is a strong fear and urge to avoid a particular object or situation. People can develop specific phobias when something very scary happens to them (a dog bites the person) or when the person repeatedly observes someone (a friend or parent) being afraid of something. In addition, people with phobias sometimes have a normal childhood fear that they just have not outgrown.

Most teens who have a specific phobia do not ask for help because it does not interfere that much with their normal routines, going to school, or friendships. People can become afraid, under the right conditions, of most anything. There are as many kinds of specific phobias as there are things and situations. The most common types of specific phobias are:

- Fear of animals (snakes, bats, spiders, bees)
- Fear of heights (high floors in buildings, top of mountains, bridges)
- Fear of flying (airplane crashes, cabin depressurizes, terrorists attack)
- Fear of doctors and dentists (medical and dental procedures)
- Fear of thunder or lightning
- Fear of blood or pain
- Fear of illness or disease

Check out Ellie's story and her fear of spiders.

*I've always, and I mean __always__, been deathly afraid of spiders. My
mom is afraid of spiders, too. It never seemed to be a big deal. Sure,
I never wore shorts, and I always slept under a heavy blanket. All
because I was afraid a spider would crawl on me, but whatever.
I was fine with it. Sometimes it would bother my family because
I could not take anything out of my closet or clean under my
bed. I made them do that because, you never know, there might
be a spider there! But the thing that bugged me and my family
the most was that I never wanted to take a vacation during the
summer—only the winter when there was less of a chance of seeing a spider wherever we visited. Even that was okay, until I
learned that my class was traveling to South America this summer.
Many of my friends were going. I wanted to go too, but then
I thought about spiders. I knew that if I didn't do something
about this fear, I would miss a ton of fun. It was starting to hold
me back.*—Ellie, age 14

SUMMING IT UP

Now, whether we call it anxiety or anxiety disorder, the goal of
this book is to help you learn to calm your anxious mind and
body. The goal is not to take away all your anxiety and fear. We
only want to help you decrease the anxiety that does not help or
protect you and that gets in your way. In other words, we want to
help you get rid of the unhelpful anxiety, the kind of anxiety that
really spins your Worry Wheel. As you work your way through
this book, you will see that we have included tools to help each
part of your Worry Wheel. You will learn breathing, relaxation,
and visualization tools in Chapter 3 (*Breathing and Relaxing*) that
you can use to calm your anxious body. In Chapter 4 (*Thinking*

Smart), you will learn tools to calm your anxious mind, and in Chapter 5 (*Facing Fears One Step at a Time*), you will learn how to change your anxious actions to slow down the Worry Wheel and get off. In addition, in Chapter 6 (*Floating With Panic Attacks*), you'll learn what to do when your Worry Wheel spins way out of control, and you have a panic attack.

CHAPTER **2**

WHO AND HOW TO ASK FOR HELP

Many of you are experts at helping others. You help your friends resolve conflicts, you help your parents with household chores, and you help your younger brothers and sisters learn to do things you can do like ride a bike or hit a home run. Even as experts at helping others, you do ask for help from time to time. You ask teachers to help you learn. You ask parents to teach you to drive. You ask friends to listen to you when you are upset. But we understand that it is still sometimes easier to give help than to ask for it. Dealing with anxiety and panic may be one of these times.

In the last chapter, we talked about when you might need to ask for help. Here we will help you understand who and how to ask for help, should you decide to do that. First, we describe common reasons teens refuse help for their anxiety and panic. We discuss the pluses of getting help as well as one important minus. In addition, we describe how you can build a support team to help you calm your anxious mind, including how to find a psychotherapist to help. Last, we answer the questions most teens ask us about psychotherapy and whether it makes sense for them to accept this kind of help.

REFUSING HELP: SIX COMMON REASONS

You might have good reasons for why you are not interested in accepting help to calm your anxious mind. You might think your anxiety is not that bad, or that you are fine just the way you are. Many teens have trouble accepting help, too. Lots of teens might think:

- It's not that bad.
- It's not that bad today.
- I'm fine just the way I am.
- It's too embarrassing to admit.
- What's the point?
- I don't want to bother people.

So before you refuse help outright, let's talk through some of the common reasons why teens would not want help and how you might think about things differently.

IT'S NOT THAT BAD. Sometimes teens deny there is a problem, or they minimize just how hard a time they are having calming their anxious minds. They might compare themselves to family members or friends they know who are anxious too and think, "My anxiety is not as bad as her anxiety." Comparing yourself in this way can make it hard to admit there is a problem because you believe that your anxiety must be extreme or that you must suffer a great deal before it is okay to accept help. This is not true. Different teens respond in different ways to anxiety. In fact, you may be coping better than a family member or friend, but still you are suffering and your anxiety may be excessive. If you are suffering, that may be reason enough to ask for help. Another reason teens have trouble accepting help is that they are used to appearing perfect in every way. They earn straight As in school. They are popular. They are captains of their teams.

They succeed at almost everything they try. Parents, friends, and teachers think of them as perfect or the best. In their minds, perfect teens do not have problems. Teens may think, "No problem. No reason to ask for help." But the truth of the matter is, just because you are doing well in many areas of your life does not mean you might not benefit from some help now and then. Furthermore, no one is perfect, and expecting this of yourself can really add to your stress and anxiety.

IT'S NOT THAT BAD TODAY. Sometimes teens feel anxious and sometimes they do not (or at least not as anxious as they felt a week ago). Anxiety fluctuates, and often these natural ups and downs can make it difficult for teens to see that their anxiety is really a problem. This is especially true when they are not feeling anxious and life seems easy. Then they think everything is fine. "Why do I need help? I'm not anxious!" However, just because your anxiety goes up and down does not mean that the anxiety is not a problem for you. Instead, think about whether your anxiety has been going up and down for many months and years, rather than up and down from day to day. Typically, anxiety and fears diminish or disappear in less than six months. If your anxiety has lingered longer than that, your anxiety may be excessive and therefore a problem.

I'M FINE JUST THE WAY I AM. Some teens have parents who think that their teen's level of anxiety is normal or acceptable and say, "You're fine just the way you are." This can happen for many reasons. Some parents are anxious themselves and think it is fine to feel anxious most of the time or to avoid certain situations and play it safe. When they see their son feeling and behaving in the same ways that they do, they think this is normal and are unaware that he has a problem.

Other parents are unsure about telling their son there is anything wrong. They believe that if they suggest to him that he has an anxiety problem, he will get upset. These parents pretend that his anxiety is normal and operate on the principle "out of sight, out of mind." In addition, parents might try to protect their daughter by making allowances or doing things for her to reduce her anxiety. For example, parents might drive their daughter to school so that she does not have to ride on public transportation, excuse her from household chores so that the she does not have to get dirty or germy, or make accommodations so that she does not have to face other situations she fears.

Finally, some parents have just one child. Parents of an only child have no comparison. Many times parents can identify a problem because a sibling has already experienced the same difficulty or sailed through a similar situation with ease, allowing a parent to know when something is not right with their teen. There are many reasons why parents tell their teens, "You're fine just the way you are." Unfortunately, this leaves some teens unaware that there may be a problem.

IT'S TOO EMBARRASSING TO ADMIT. Let's face it, no one likes to admit that they have a problem. For some teens, they feel so much shame or embarrassment about being anxious that they do not want to admit there is a problem. Teens can feel defective or abnormal when they compare themselves to their friends who appear to have it all—lots of friends, good grades, and a great life—all of which seems to come easy to them. This makes it hard for an anxious teen to confess that his life is not great and that there is a problem. Many times teens are embarrassed by what they do (or do not do) because they are anxious. Perhaps he has to call a parent several times a day to check in, or he refuses to use the restroom at school or in other public places. Teens try hard to hide these behaviors from their friends, but if found out, they make light of the behavior by calling themselves "quirky" or take on the role of the funny, weird one even though they are quite ashamed and wish things were different.

WHAT'S THE POINT? Some teens have had anxiety for such a long time that they do not believe that there is anything that they can do to help themselves. Perhaps in the past, a teen's parents encouraged her on several occasions to try a sleepover, but each time, she ended up making an excuse and coming home. Perhaps a teen tried to face his fear on his own but he was unable to follow through. Nothing is more demoralizing to teens than to try and try and not quite make it. After a while, teens give up. At other times, teens believe they have so many worries and fears that there is no chance they will be able to succeed in their lifetime. Or even if they conquer a fear, it will not do much good as there are so many more to tackle. This attitude can really get a teen down. However, a teen's past attempts may have failed because she did not have the right tools or because she believed that a small step or success in the right direction did not mean much.

I DON'T WANT TO BOTHER PEOPLE. Some anxious teens feel like they rely too much on friends and family to help them cope with anxiety. But really, these teens do not rely on friends and family enough! They are reluctant to ask for help because they worry that they will put others off or upset them if they request their help. Teens who do not want to bother other people may think that asking parents or friends for help will burden them with their problems or that their anxiety is so extreme that it will overwhelm them. However, nothing could be farther from the truth. Most parents and friends often feel honored when asked to help a teen learn and apply tools to manage anxiety. Parents and friends much prefer helping in this way rather than providing a lot of reassurance to calm the anxious teen or doing all the things he is unable to do because of his anxiety.

At other times, teens confuse asking for help with demanding help and do not want to come off looking needy. Once again, this rarely happens. In fact, teens can unintentionally appear needy when they do <u>not</u> get help. But when they do ask for help, they appear courageous.

Although it might be hard to accept help, it is okay to ask for it. Everyone asks for help from time to time. A musician might ask for an extra rehearsal or sit in with another musician to warm up or to get some support before a performance or a recording session. An actor might consult with a dialect coach to prepare for a new role in a movie or television show. A professional basketball player might ask a teammate for help with her jump shot. Asking others to help may not look like an option for you, but we hope that you will see that it can be (or at least consider it as a possibility).

RECEIVING HELP: PLUSES AND MINUSES

Like most things in life, there are pluses and minuses to asking for and getting help. The first plus of accepting help to calm your anxious mind is that you will feel less alone. For example, some teens opt out of social opportunities because they think, "I'll embarrass myself" or "I'm afraid I'll have another panic attack." Other teens worry excessively about their grades, stay home, and study all the time. These teens miss doing fun things with friends, but worse yet, they suffer with their anxious minds alone and often in silence.

The second plus is that telling the right people that you have a problem with anxiety can be the first step toward developing a plan to calm your anxious mind. Parents, psychotherapists, teachers, and friends can help you set goals, practice tools, or praise your efforts to calm your anxious mind.

The final plus of accepting help is that you may gather additional support for learning and practicing the tools in this book.

Sometimes, you may not think to use a tool, but it can help if a friend or family member gently reminds you to take a calming breath or to think differently in a stressful situation. Some of the tools are difficult to practice, such as facing a fear, and a support person can help you hang in there and succeed. As you will see later in this book, a team and a plan are essential in order to calm your anxious mind and keep it calm over time.

Although there are pluses to telling others about your anxious mind, there is an important minus, too. Once you tell someone about your anxious mind you cannot control what the person does with that information. On occasion, a friend, a teacher, or even a parent can misunderstand what it means when you say you are anxious. Friends might not include you in certain activities or might not ask you to hang out with them because they are overly concerned that it will stress you out or make things harder for you. Teachers might think that you are trying to get out of schoolwork by using your anxious mind as an excuse. Parents might over-react and think you are too fragile to do anything or under-react and think that you are making things worse than they really are. These responses are not helpful or accurate and are likely to make you feel worse about yourself.

When considering the pluses and minuses of telling someone about your anxious mind, we want you to think carefully through how a person will handle this information before you tell her, so that you are ready to correct quickly any misunderstandings the person may have. Still, some people, no matter what you say, will misunderstand what it means to have an anxious mind. Perhaps these people are not the best people to help you. If this is the case, we hope you will consider seeking help from someone else. If you are in psychotherapy, your psychotherapist may be able to help you sort this out for yourself or suggest who might be the best people to share this important information.

BUILDING MY SUPPORT TEAM

Once you have decided to ask for help, you will want to choose a few people to become part of the team that works together to help you calm your anxious mind. Consider both a support person and a trained mental health professional for your team. The support person can help you locate a trained mental health professional to join your team and support you as you learn and practice the tools in this book. Think of the support person as a cheerleader who encourages you from the sidelines, particularly when you are struggling or perhaps feeling a bit too frightened to try the next step of your plan. Many teens choose someone they already know and trust to be their support person, such as a parent or school counselor.

A mental health professional is an important member of your team, too. This person will already know many of the tools in this book and, ideally, will have had experience helping other anxious teens learn and use them. A mental health professional can be a counselor, a psychologist, or a psychiatrist and may work in a clinic, hospital, school, or private office. Think of this person as a coach who not only provides direction from the sidelines, but who also gets in the game and teaches you strategies and tools as well as helps you develop a step-by-step plan to tackle your anxiety and panic.

Find a Support Person

Although there is no such thing as a perfect support person, choosing someone who cares about you and your well-being is perhaps the most important quality. For many teens, their support person is typically an adult such as a parent, family member, teacher, school counselor, pastor, rabbi, or priest. However, you might prefer to enlist the help of a mature and trusted sibling, friend, boyfriend, or girlfriend who can provide peer-to-peer support. You could call in extra support from a parent when you need an adult to make calls to an insurance company or to schedule a first psychotherapy appointment, for example. The following list of criteria can help you determine whether someone is ready to be your support person. The more criteria the person meets, the better! Ask yourself, is my support person someone who

- Is available to me in person, by e-mail, or by phone when I need some support?
- Is willing to listen to what I have to say rather than assuming that my concerns are trivial?
- Is familiar with my particular situation and is willing and able to keep this information private, so long as I am safe?
- Treats me with dignity and respect and sees that my anxious mind is only one part of me, not the whole me?
- Is willing to help me find local resources including a trained mental health professional or support group?

After reading these criteria, can you think of someone who might be good as your support person? Once you have chosen your support person, the next step is to figure out how to approach him and what to say. Begin by picking a time when you can talk with him face-to-face, although phone or e-mail can be a backup option, too. Next, ensure that you have some privacy and at least 30 minutes to discuss fully your situation. Finally, outline what you want to tell him about your anxiety. You will want to

- Introduce your anxiety problem.
- Explain how it has become a problem.
- Get a commitment from the person to help you.

I HAVE AN ANXIOUS MIND. First, you will introduce the topic. Convey that you have something important and personal you want to share. Make it clear that this information is private and tell your support person whom he can tell or not tell. Let your support person know that you are struggling with anxiety.

MY ANXIETY HAS BECOME A PROBLEM. Next, you will want to explain in some detail how your anxiety has become a problem. Describe how you have been feeling and how anxiety is interfering in your life. For example, if you have stopped doing things or going places because you are anxious, tell the support person about this. Are your grades dropping or are friends telling you that you worry too much? Is your sleep or appetite affected? Finally, explain to the support person how long this has been happening and what you have done to manage your anxiety including what has and has not worked.

WILL YOU BE ABLE TO BE MY SUPPORT PERSON? At the end of the conversation, get a commitment from him to help you. Explain to him that you would like some help from him and from a professional. Then, explain how he can assist you.

Your discussion might look something like this:

I want to talk to you about something important. I'd really like it if you could keep this just between us, since I don't want Julia to find out. I definitely don't want my friends or teachers to know. I think I have more anxiety and stress than I can handle on my own, and I've started having anxiety attacks. I get really anxious whenever I have to talk in front of others at school, and I have started to have these anxiety attacks when I am out on the weekends with friends. I even get this way when I think about going out. It's been hard to sleep at night, and I can't focus in class because I'm worrying about looking like an idiot in front of everyone. This has been going on for a few months now. At first, I thought it would go away, but it hasn't and I really want to feel better. Could you help me to find a professional who I can talk to about this?

If you invite someone to become your support person and he declines, try not to become too discouraged. Consider who else might be qualified for the role and ask her. Once you have found a support person who has the time and skills to help, ask her to help you find a trained mental health professional. This will get the ball rolling and is the first step in getting the help you need.

Locate a Professional

Telling a complete stranger all about your anxiety and your greatest fears can seem, well, scary! Many teens feel anxious when first meeting a psychotherapist, particularly if they have never discussed their worries and fears with someone they did not know. In fact, many teens have told us that they had second thoughts about coming in to talk to us for the first time or that they had doubts that psychotherapy would even help them. However, we hope you will not let your anxiety and reservations stand in the way of getting help. Working with a psychotherapist who can teach you practical and effective tools—like the tools described in this book—can be an important part of the plan to help you calm your anxious mind.

To lessen some of the anxiety you might have about starting psychotherapy, you will want to know that the person is the right psychotherapist to help you. At the first meeting, it is okay to ask the psychotherapist whether she has the qualifications to help you with your anxiety. In addition, it is important that you feel comfortable with the psychotherapist and clearly understand your role and her role in helping you. To ensure that the psychotherapist is qualified to help you, ask her these questions:

- Is your professional training in medicine, counseling, social work, or psychology?
- Do you have experience working with adolescents?

- Do you have experience treating anxiety and anxiety disorders?
- Will you keep personal information private and share it only with the people you feel are essential to inform?
- Will you help me set clear goals for calming my anxious mind that are realistic and make sense to me?
- Will you be open to feedback from me about ways to improve the psychotherapy if I believe it is not helping?

Once you have decided you are ready to start psychotherapy, you will want to locate a trained mental health professional. If you live in a large city or densely populated area, it will likely be easy for you to find a qualified mental health professional. However, if you live in a rural area or small community, it may be a bit more difficult. Here are some ideas that may help you find the right person:

- Talk to your physician or school counselor for a referral to a child and adolescent psychotherapist.
- Call your insurance company for a referral to a psychotherapist on your insurance panel.
- Use online resources such as the Yellow Pages (www.yellowpages.com) or other *find-a-psychotherapist* Web sites like the American Psychological Association (www.apa.org), the Academy of Cognitive Therapy (www.academyofct.org), or the Association of Behavioral and Cognitive Therapies (www.abct.org). Check for additional resources at the end of this book.
- Talk to other adults who might know qualified psychotherapists in your area.

Many teens who are considering psychotherapy for the first time are often uncertain about what to expect during the first meeting. Do not assume that psychotherapy and psychotherapists look like what you see on television or in the movies! Although often funny, these portrayals are seldom accurate, particularly when it comes to a psychotherapy focused on teaching you tools to calm your anxious mind.

To help you prepare, look at some typical questions teens have about psychotherapy and the answers we give.

Frequently Asked Questions About Psychotherapy

Question: Will I have to take tests or have a physical exam for the therapist to know what is wrong with me?

Answer: Probably not. Some doctors and psychotherapists might want you to fill out questionnaires to help them understand more about you and your situation, whereas others might prefer to gather this information simply by asking you questions and taking notes, similar to an interview. Obtaining this information helps them to understand what is going on and to come up with the best treatment plan for you. Sometimes, however, your doctor is a psychiatrist who can prescribe medication. Before he gives you any medication, your psychiatrist might want you to have some medical tests or to give you a physical exam to determine whether you are healthy and make certain you do not have a medical condition that could cause you to have anxiety-like symptoms. Taking these steps ensures your psychiatrist can safely prescribe medication.

Question: Will the doctor tell my parents, teachers, or other people about what I say?

Answer: There is a term called *confidentiality* that protects what information a psychotherapist can share with other people. However, because you are a minor until you turn 18, your parents have the legal right to talk to your doctor without your consent or permission. Therefore, we recommend you discuss this with your parents and your psychotherapist when you start psychotherapy, so that you can decide together what information is private—between you and your psychotherapist—and what information she can share with your parents, teachers, or other people.

(continued)

Frequently Asked Questions About Psychotherapy
(continued)

Question: Will I have to take medication?

Answer: Some doctors might recommend you take medication in addition to receiving counseling or psychotherapy. Talk this over with your doctor and your parents so that you understand why the doctor is recommending medication in addition to psychotherapy.

Question: How long do I have to meet with the psychotherapist?

Answer: The number of meetings can vary from a few (fewer than 10 sessions) to many (20 sessions or more). You and your psychotherapist will decide how long to meet based on your specific situation and how anxiety affects your life, as well as what you want to accomplish in your psychotherapy.

Question: What if I do not like the psychotherapist?

Answer: We hope you will like the psychotherapist enough to attend a few sessions to determine if the psychotherapist can help you. If after several meetings you really do not connect, talk to your parents or even to the psychotherapist to see if you can figure out why this is happening and to determine if it would be better for you to work with someone else.

Question: What makes a psychotherapist better able to help me than someone whom I already know and trust?

Answer: Although people you know and trust and even love can be a great support when you are struggling, they sometimes have other roles and responsibilities that can get in the way of them being fully available to you. In addition, it is not easy for a friend or parent to be completely objective when it comes to advising you. The job of the psychotherapist is to place your interests and well-being first and to be as objective as she or he can in advising you. In addition, a psychotherapist experienced in helping anxious teens will know which tools and what kind of advice are the most effective and helpful. Although well meaning, friends or parents can sometimes suggest things that actually will make your anxiety and panic worse.

MOVING FORWARD

Learning to calm your anxious mind is hard work and even more difficult if you believe that you have to do it alone. Seeking and accepting the right kind of help can feel scary but is often an important step toward easing your anxiety. Even if you do not accept help now, knowing that it is available can make you feel less anxious and more hopeful that things can be different for you.

In this chapter, we presented six common reasons that teens refuse help, and we stepped through the pluses and minuses of getting help so that you can decide whether accepting help at this time is the right thing for you. In addition, we described how to go about identifying and inviting a support person and a psychotherapist to join your team to help you calm your anxious mind. If you need a little more time to think things through, take it. Feel free to look through this chapter again, particularly the pluses and minuses of getting help. The right team can make a big difference in how quickly you learn to calm your anxious mind. Good luck!

CHAPTER 3

BREATHING AND RELAXING

Have you ever watched LeBron James at the free throw line? He takes one, two, perhaps even three slow deep breaths that calm his body and mind as he bounces the ball several times. Then he stops, focuses intently on the basket, visualizing the ball swooshing through the hoop, and then shoots. He usually makes a clean shot. In a similar way, Yo-Yo Ma, the classical cellist, might squeeze his fists or shrug his shoulders to release tension before beginning to play. These actions may seem small and insignificant, but consider this: deep breathing and muscle relaxation allows LeBron James and Yo-Yo Ma to remain calm and focused, which is a big part of what enables them to produce some amazing results.

Learning to relax and calm your body in any situation is the first step toward learning to calm your anxious mind. Breathing is so automatic most of us are unaware we are doing it. But have you noticed how your breathing changes when stress and anxiety hits your body? When you feel stressed or anxious, you breathe faster, also known as hyperventilation, which causes you to inhale more oxygen than you need, triggering an imbalance between the oxygen and carbon dioxide in the blood. This causes the blood vessels to tighten up and prevents a sufficient amount of oxygen from reaching organs and cells. All this really means is that you can experience sensations of dizziness, tingling, and light-headedness that are completely harmless, but can feel weird or scary and really start your Worry Wheel spinning. In addition, when you breathe too fast, your muscles can tense up, causing you to feel tired and sore. Even if you are not breathing fast but are feeling stressed or anxious, your muscles tense. The longer you feel anxious, the more tense your muscles get.

You can calm your anxious body by learning how to handle rapid and anxious breathing, relax your muscles, and quiet your mind. This chapter will teach you how to do all of this by using three important Calm Body tools—abdominal breathing, progressive muscle relaxation, and visualization. We include directions and tips in each section to help you incorporate these tools into your daily life, allowing you to begin to slow down your Worry Wheel. These tools are an important part of a successful plan to calm your anxious mind, and they are easy to learn and even easier to practice. With breathing, relaxation, and visualization tools, you can quickly reduce your body's stress and anxiety. Once your body is a bit calmer, you will be better able to use other tools described in this book.

USING CALM BODY TOOLS

Breathing, relaxation, and visualization practice works best if there are no distractions to get in the way. Find a quiet place to go for 10–15 minutes where no one will interrupt you. Turn off the TV, phone, computer, and music. Make sure there are no other loud noises, too.

Next, find time in your day to practice. You will likely want to schedule some time. You might be thinking, "Yeah right, that's impossible," but think for a minute. Is there a time when things are less hectic for you or when you can take a short break? This might be right after school but before you start homework. Or maybe it could be planned as the first thing on the weekend or right before dinner on Sunday night. Choosing a time that works best for you will make it easier to learn and apply these skills every day, helping you to become an expert at calming your anxious body. Make this practice a priority.

When I first heard about breathing and relaxing tools, I thought they were for people who do yoga and meditation. I also was afraid people could tell if I was practicing them. However, it turns out that all sorts of people use these tools everyday, and they're easy to use without anyone being wise to what you're doing.

—Bobbie, age 15

Abdominal Breathing

Abdominal breathing is the first Calm Body tool. To practice abdominal breathing with a calm mind, go to your quiet spot, close the door, and get comfortable in a comfy chair or lie down. Make sure you are wearing loose clothing and uncross your legs and arms.

Begin by imagining you have a red balloon attached to the end of a long thin tube that starts in your nose or mouth and ends in your stomach. Place your hand on your stomach over your belly button and feel how that balloon inflates and deflates in rhythm with the rise and fall of your stomach. Close your eyes and keep your hand resting on your stomach as you slowly breathe in and out. Take a slow deep breath of air in through your nose as you count to three (one–two–three). Pause and hold it for the count of three. Then slowly breathe out for the count of three.

As you repeat this, picture the red balloon inflating as you inhale and deflating as you exhale. Focus on the air traveling in and out *slowly* and *evenly*. Slow calming breaths will decrease muscle tension and lower your anxiety. Take another slow deep breath in through your nose as you count to three. Hold it for three counts and release for three counts. Pause for a moment and inhale for three counts. Hold for three counts and exhale for three counts. Pause.

On the next inhale, slowly say to yourself, "Calm," stretching out the letters while you picture the word in your mind's eye. Hold your breath for three counts and as you exhale, say to yourself, "Mind," stretching out the letters while you imagine the word in your mind's eye. Repeat this.

Repeat and continue this slow, calm, and rhythmic breathing for another 5–10 minutes for a total practice time of 10–15 minutes. If your mind wanders during the exercise, just refocus your attention by picturing the word "Calm" or "Mind" and continue breathing in and out, noticing your stomach rise and fall.

To review, here are the steps:

1. Breathe in through your nose and out through your mouth (unless your doctor or parent has suggested that you should not do this due to medical reasons). If you cannot breathe through your nose, you can do all the breathing through your mouth.
2. Breathe in slowly as you imagine the word "Calm," stretching out the letters throughout your inhale.
3. Pause for the count of three.
4. Breathe out slowly as you imagine the word "Mind," stretching out the letters throughout your exhale.
5. Rest for the count of three.
6. Repeat this pattern for a total time of 10–15 minutes.

Progressive Muscle Relaxation

Progressive muscle relaxation is the second Calm Body tool and is an important tool to reduce body tension. As mentioned above, the classic cellist Yo-Yo Ma works to release the tension in his hands prior to and during performances. Professional athletes such as Eli Manning and Serena Williams have tricks to relax their muscles before a game. Have you ever noticed how Eli Manning and the rest of the New York Giants shrug their shoulders or pump their fists during the game? Or how Serena Williams and other tennis players crouch over and hop from one foot to another before a serve? These gestures allow the players to release pent up tension, which helps their muscles perform optimally.

Just like famous musicians and athletes, you can learn to relax your muscles and decrease unwanted tension and anxiety. Begin by sitting or lying down with your arms by your side and your legs uncrossed out in front of you. Close your eyes. Start by squeezing your eyes tight. Then scrunch your nose as if you have smelled a rotten egg and pull the edges of your mouth back toward your ears into a forced smile. Then, bite down to tense your mouth and jaw. Hold this position for the count of 15. Then slowly release your eyes, nose, mouth, and jaw for another 15 seconds. Relax your face so that all the wrinkles disappear. Your face will be smooth and relaxed, your cheeks will feel soft, and your tongue will be loose in your mouth. Notice how different this feels from when your face was tight and tense. If you learn the difference, you can make your muscles relax when you notice they are tense.

Now, move to your neck and shoulders. Tuck your neck into your shoulders like a scared turtle. Hold this position for 15 seconds, observing the pull on your neck muscles and the discomfort you feel. Now release and let your shoulders drop down and your head relax. Hold this position for 15 seconds.

Next, move on to the hands and arms. Make fists with your hands and cross your arms at the wrists. Hold your arms up in front of you and push them together as if you are arm wrestling with yourself. Hold your arms in this position with your fists clenched for 15 seconds. Then let your fists uncurl and your arms slowly fall to your side. Hold this position for 15 seconds. Your arms might feel like wet spaghetti. Observe how your arms are feeling loose and heavy. This sensation of relaxation feels much better than when your muscles are tense and tight.

Next, pull your arms behind your back and try to make your elbows touch. Hold this position for 15 seconds and then release.

Next, suck in your stomach, making your abdomen get hard and tight. Clench your buttock muscles together. Hold this position for 15 seconds. Notice how the tension feels uncomfortable. Then release and let your stomach go out farther and farther while you release your buttock muscles. Do this for 15 seconds. You might notice as you go through all of these muscle exercises, tensing and relaxing, that you are starting to feel more relaxed. Your muscles might feel heavy and calm, and your whole body is beginning to feel relaxed. You are in charge of how your body feels and you are commanding your muscles to relax.

The last exercise is for the legs and feet. Stick your legs straight out in front of you and direct your toes towards your nose while you scrunch your toes into a tight ball. Hold for 15 seconds and then release for 15 seconds. Your legs might feel loose and floppy as they begin to feel relaxed.

You have now gone through all six muscle groups. You can repeat these six steps several times to relax your body even more, beginning again with your eyes.

Briefly, here is the routine for progressive muscle relaxation:

1. Begin with your eyes, nose, mouth, and jaw (face), alternating between tightening and tensing for 15 seconds and then relaxing for 15 seconds.
2. Keep the rest of your body and muscles relaxed. Move through the next five muscle groups one group at a time:
   - Neck and shoulders
   - Hands and arms
   - Upper back
   - Abdomen and buttocks
   - Legs and feet
3. Pay attention to how different your muscles feel when they are tense versus when they are relaxed, noticing how the sensation of relaxation feels better than the sensation of tension.
4. Repeat the six muscle groups if you want to relax more.

Remember, do not engage in these exercises if your doctor or parent does not think the exercise is okay for you because of medical reasons.

Visualization

Visualization is the final Calm Body tool in this chapter. It is a method to reduce tension and anxiety. Actors and athletes, among other professionals, use visualization to remain calm and enhance their performance. Tiger Woods prepares to hit the ball by using visualization. On the tee box, Tiger looks down the fairway and visualizes where he wants to hit the ball. Later, when he steps onto the green, he examines the grade of the green from multiple angles. Then, just before he putts the ball, he imagines the ball rolling across the green and into the cup. Golf is a game that requires extreme mental focus, and being able to visualize your results ahead of time can make a big difference in how you play. You can learn to use and apply visualization in your daily life to calm your anxious mind and body and to enhance your focus and attention.

To practice developing your visualization tool, begin by thinking of a favorite, calm memory or of a peaceful place like floating on an inflatable raft in a warm pool or lying on the beach on a sunny day. Use all of your senses. What do you see? Look for the colors, shapes, people, or animals near you and far away.

Now what do you hear? Are there birds chirping or waves crashing? Are there any smells like the ocean or freshly cut grass? Can you taste anything? Imagine that you are walking closer to the sea and tasting some of the salt water or taking a sip of that ice-cold lemonade.

Lastly, how do things feel? Touch a soft flower petal or a hard rock and notice the texture. As you are imagining this, you may notice that upsetting or anxious thoughts or images might force their way into your beautiful scene. Don't try to ignore these thoughts, as they will only get louder or more intrusive. Instead, let them pass through the scene like a gentle breeze.

I treat intrusive, annoying thoughts like a nosey neighbor. I say "Hey, anxious thought. I'm busy and can't chat now." Or I imagine folding the thought into a paper airplane. I throw it into the air and watch it fly away from my calm scene.

—Bobbie, age 15

Continue to sit with this image for at least 5–10 minutes, noticing how peaceful it feels and enjoy a sense of calm and the absence of anxiety and tension.

Visualization is a powerful tool. Here is how to practice:

1. Find a quiet place and lie comfortably on your back.
2. Close your eyes.
3. Think of a calm place you like to visit. It does not have to be a location you have actually visited, but can be somewhere you would like to go. Use your imagination! You can create an imaginary place, too.
4. Use all your senses (sight, smell, hearing, taste, and touch) to enhance the experience and to explore fully your scene.
5. Notice how you feel in your body. Pay attention to how your muscles are relaxing, how your heart rate and breathing are slowing, and how your mind is quieting and focusing its energy on the images you are creating.

DEVELOPING A SCRIPT

Abdominal breathing, muscle relaxation, and visualization are three important Calm Body tools you can use to help manage your tense and anxious body. We encourage you to be creative in how you use these tools including combining them into a single routine. You can also modify your environment by dimming the lights and playing some soothing music to enhance your experience as you use these tools. Once you have a routine that you like, create your own personalized script. You can find an example of a script at the end of this section.

When your script is ready, it really helps to burn it onto a CD or rip it to your MP3 player. Then you can practice it anytime and anywhere. For some teens, it helps to practice these tools with another person such as a friend, parent, or psychotherapist. Regardless of whether you chose to practice alone or with another person, begin by practicing for 10–15 minutes once or twice daily for two to four weeks until using these tools is easy and automatic. Then you are ready to use your Calm Body tools when you find yourself stuck on the Worry Wheel. Some common situations in which you can use your script include:

- Before tests, performances, or athletic events.
- When you are having trouble falling asleep.
- At the onset of or during a panic attack.
- When you are stressed out thinking about all you have to do.
- When you notice your muscles are tight and tense.
- Before going on a date or engaging in a social situation that causes you anxiety.
- At any time you find you are stuck on the Worry Wheel.

Ellie's Calm Body and Mind Script

This is the script I created by combining the three Calm Body tools discussed in this chapter. I recorded this myself and listen to my script right before I go to sleep. You can use my script or modify the words to make one of your own.

- Lie down on your bed and shake out your muscles to get comfortable.
- Close your eyes and imagine a red balloon attached to the end of a long thin tube that starts in your nose or mouth and ends in your stomach.
- Place your hand on your stomach right over your belly button to feel the balloon inflate and deflate in rhythm with the rise and fall of your stomach.
- Now, take a slow deep breath of air in through your nose as you count to three (one–two–three). Pause and hold it for the count of three. Then slowly breathe out on the count of three. Repeat.
- After a few breath cycles, insert the word "Calm" on the inhale breath and "Peace" on the exhale breath.
- Continue to do this for 10–15 additional breath cycles, paying attention to the slow rise and fall of your stomach.

Ellie's Calm Body and Mind Script *(continued)*

- Notice how good it feels to start to slow down your breathing. Remember, slow breaths will help to calm your anxious mind and body.
- Now, squeeze your eyes tight, scrunch your nose, and smile hard as you pull the edges of your mouth back toward your ears. Bite down to tense your mouth and jaw. Hold this position and count to 15.
- Slowly release your eyes, nose, mouth, and jaw and count to 15 again.
- Notice as you relax your face that the wrinkles disappear, like melting snow, leaving your skin smooth and relaxed. Your cheeks feel soft and your tongue is loose in your mouth. Notice how different this feels from when your face was tight and tense. It feels much better to feel relaxed instead of tense and tight.
- Now, focus your attention on your neck and shoulders. Tuck your neck into your shoulders. Hold this position for a count of 15 (one–two–three–four . . .), feeling the pull on your neck muscles and the discomfort you may feel.
- Now release these muscles and let your shoulders drop down, relaxing your head. Your head might feel heavy or floppy as it relaxes. Hold this relaxed pose for a count of 15.
- Shift your focus to your hands and arms by making fists with your hands and crossing your arms at your wrists. Stick your arms up in front of your body and push them together as if you're arm wrestling with yourself. Hold your arms in this position with your fists clenched for a count of 15.
- Let your fists uncurl and your arms slowly fall to your side and hold this position for a count of 15. Notice how your arms feel loose and heavy. A feeling of relaxation is spreading through your body. Last of all, pull your arms behind your back and try to make your elbows touch. Hold this position for a count of 15 and then release for a count of 15.
- With your calm breathing and your relaxed muscles, begin to take your mind to a peaceful place. Imagine that you are lying on a quiet, empty beach. Feel the warm sun on your back, and the grainy sand under your hands. Look out toward the sea, and notice turquoise water and small white waves. The sound of the seagulls calling to one another is shrill against the quiet of this empty beach. Smell the scent of tropical flowers

(continued)

45

Ellie's Calm Body and Mind Script *(continued)*

drifting toward you from a nearby garden. Reach down and take a sip of ice-cold mango juice from your glass.

- As you experience all of these sensations, notice a calm, peaceful feeling and realize that worry and anxiety are far away.
- Begin your slow deep breathing cycles again saying, "Calm" as you inhale and "Peace" as you exhale.
- Continue your rhythmic breathing for 5–10 repetitions while continuing to imagine the beautiful, warm sandy beach scene.
- Enjoy this peaceful and relaxing state for as long as you like.

PRACTICING YOUR CALM BODY TOOLS

Re-training your mind and body to feel relaxed will take time. Like most of the things you do, practice is how you become good at something, whether you are learning to play the piano or to shoot free throws. Daily practice will help you learn a new skill quickly, so decide on a time where you will be free from distraction and can listen to your recording or read your script. Some teens like to do this right before they leave for school or last thing before bed at night. There is no right time, just the time that is right for you. To help remind you to practice daily, use the Relaxation Log. For each day of the week, record which Calm Body tool you used and the level of anxiety and relaxation you felt during the practice session. The Relaxation Log can help you to track your level of anxiety and relaxation over time. Watch as your anxiety rating decreases and your relaxation rating increases as you practice. Soon you will be able to relax without using your script or recording, even in the middle of class or in other public settings.

My Relaxation Log

	CALM BODY TOOLS	ANXIETY RATING	RELAXATION RATING
MONDAY			
TUESDAY			
WEDNESDAY			
THURSDAY			
FRIDAY			
SATURDAY			
SUNDAY			

Rating scale: 0 = not at all; 10 = extremely.
Calm Body tools: abdominal breathing; progressive muscle relaxation; visualization.

THINKING SMART

Have you ever noticed that people view the same event differently? Imagine that your teacher announces a field trip to a nearby city. At first glance, it would seem that your class would view this as a chance to get out of school, making everyone feel happy and excited. However, upon closer inspection, some teens might not view the trip as such a great thing. One teen might dislike being away from friends and her regular school routine and think, "I don't like field trips. I'll be stuck with my class and I'll miss being with my friends. I won't get to hang out at lunch." Another teen might think, "I can't be with my friends, but at least I won't have to be in chemistry class." Or another teen who is anxious about taking the subway might think, "It won't be safe. I'll freak out and humiliate myself." In all these instances, the situation is the same, but the teens' responses and feelings are different because of how they think about going on the trip.

The goal of this chapter is to understand how anxious thoughts influence behaviors and emotions. You will learn how to identify, evaluate, and change unhelpful anxious self-talk to reach a final goal of "thinking smart and acting brave." We will begin with a description of the A-B-C Model of anxiety and examine how anxious self-talk maintains anxiety, fear, and avoidance. The chapter highlights typical styles of anxious self-talk (problematic thoughts, beliefs, and assumptions) that contribute to excessive anxiety and fear, and we will present several Calm Mind tools you can use to evaluate and change anxious self-talk into self-talk that will calm your anxious mind.

UNDERSTANDING SELF-TALK AND ANXIETY

We call what we think and what we say to ourselves *self-talk*. It is one way we interpret situations, and those interpretations can determine how we feel and act. You have the capacity to generate many types of self-talk, and each type can be helpful, neutral, or unhelpful. You might be surprised to learn that even anxious self-talk can be helpful at times. For example, imagine you are about to cross the street, and just as you step off the curb, you hear the rev of an engine and squealing tires. You instantly generate the self-talk statement "Danger," and your body swings into high alert. Your heart races, you experience a surge of adrenaline, and your reflexes act instantly to avoid danger. You stop and brace yourself. The speeding car narrowly misses you. This example of anxious self-talk is helpful, as it protects you from danger.

But anxious self-talk can also be unhelpful. What if every time you step off a curb you think, "Don't cross, it's dangerous," even when the road is empty and the situation safe? This example of anxious self-talk is unhelpful as the situation is safe or that danger is very unlikely. Unfortunately, anxious teens have way too much unhelpful anxious self-talk which contributes to unnecessary fear and avoidance and lots of anxiety.

DECODING ANXIOUS SELF-TALK: THE A-B-C MODEL

Self-talk is so automatic that it is easy to believe the initial situation is what is making you feel anxious, when really it is how you interpret or what you think about the situation that triggers your feelings and actions. Another way to understand the effects of self-talk is with a simple model called the A-B-C Model. A situation or event, called an *Activating event (A)* can create different feelings and actions known as *Consequences (C)*. This is a direct result of what you *Believe (B)* or think about the event. What the A-B-C Model demonstrates is that it is not the event that makes you feel and act the way you do, otherwise the equation would be: A→C. Instead, the beliefs and thoughts (self-talk) are what contribute to your feelings and the actions you take. For example, Bobbie and his friends are discussing plans for a summer camping trip (A). Bobbie generates this self-talk: "It's going be so awkward. I can't kayak. I'll make a fool of myself" (B). Although he agrees to go on the trip, he feels anxious (C). Instead of doing something fun like kayaking, he brings some books to read (C).

During anxious episodes, you generate lots of self-talk that can play in your mind like music tracks on a CD or songs in a playlist. In fact, anxious minds tend to have a whole collection of these that can get stuck in repeat mode, playing over and over and making you feel more and more on edge, worried, or nervous. Since anxious self-talk plays in the mind just like songs or music tracks, we use the term *tracks* to refer to anxious self-talk. Do anxious tracks play in your mind? Maybe you play things like, "I'll die of embarrassment" or "I'll never pass the test." Or maybe you think, "I won't be able to handle it." Although you have other types of self-talk stored in your collection, it may seem as if these anxious ones are always playing at high volume. They play so often it is as if they have become the soundtrack to your life, and they keep you anxious and afraid, causing you to miss fun activities and unique experiences.

The good news is that you can learn to remix your unhelpful anxious tracks. The first step is to learn how to identify when these tracks play and to understand how they make you feel and act. You can do this by creating an A-B-C-D-E Log like the one at the end of the chapter. First, think back to your most recent anxious episode. Where were you? What were you doing? Write down where you were and what you were doing in the A column. Next, in the B column, write down your anxious tracks. What was going through your anxious mind just before or during the event? Finally, write down what you were feeling or what happened in the C column. Rate how you felt (anxious, afraid, or embarrassed) from 0 (not at all strong) to 10 (the strongest ever). Leave the D and E columns blank for now. We will tell you how to use them later in the chapter.

Over the next few days and weeks, use the A, B, and C columns in the A-B-C-D-E Log to jot down several events (A) that generate anxious tracks. Be sure to record exactly what is going through your mind like, "What if I'm late and everyone laughs at me?" (B) as well as how the anxious tracks made you feel and act (C).

CLASSIFYING ANXIOUS SELF-TALK

You might think that your mind plays anxious tracks at random. However, imagine that your tracks belong on a particular CD or on a specific playlist. Just like there are different genres of music such as Rap, Reggae, Rock-n-Roll, or Country-Western, you will begin to see that your anxious tracks come in a variety of styles, too. Some teens have many styles of anxious tracks in their collection whereas other teens have just a few. Some styles are about predicting the future or guessing what others think. Other styles are about playing it safe and staying home, because you believe danger is lurking around every corner. It does not matter whether you have just a few or many styles of anxious tracks. What matters is that you become familiar with the particular styles in your collection. Once you become skilled at identifying and classifying your anxious tracks, you can then begin to evaluate and change them into tracks that will calm your anxious mind. Although we have included some basic ideas for changing anxious tracks in the style list below, we will discuss specific steps for doing this in the next section. The following is a list of styles of anxious tracks that are common for many teens.

Book Ends

Book Ends refers to a style of anxious track that suggests that there are only two possible consequences—one way or another completely opposite way with no possible outcomes in between. You might think, "I'll either ace this test or completely flunk it." However, if you have studied, you are more likely to score somewhere in the middle. You do not ace the test, but you do not flunk it either. Most of life is somewhere in the middle. Things are neither horrible nor perfect. If Book Ends is the style of track that tends to play most often in your anxious mind, try reaching for a book in the middle of the shelf rather than at either end.

Binocular Vision

When you look through binoculars at one end, everything looks bigger. But if you look through the other end, everything looks smaller. *Binocular Vision* is a type of anxious track in which you either magnify or shrink the effect of what you fear might happen. When you magnify, you expect the worst to happen or you blow things out of proportion. You might think, "If I get an F on this quiz,

I'll fail the class and I'll never get into college." In this example, you take the F and magnify or build it into a more dire consequence. Shrinking, on the other hand, makes everything look smaller. This occurs when you ignore the positives and do not give yourself any credit. You think, "It doesn't count if I get into other colleges. If I don't get into Harvard, my life is over." In this example, you minimize how getting into any college is a good accomplishment and only focus on the importance of getting into one specific college. You shrink it. If your style is Binocular Vision, try looking through regular glasses to prevent magnifying or shrinking.

Fortune Telling

Fortune Telling is a style of anxious track that convinces you that you know or can predict the future. This might be terrific if you could actually do it! Although you might be able to predict some things like, "My mom won't serve us ice cream and cake for dinner tonight," most of the time you cannot predict things very well. If the Fortune Telling style of track plays long and loud in your anxious mind, you typically predict one disaster after another. For example, you think, "I'm not going to get the job." Instead, remind yourself that even if some of your past predictions came true, it is more likely due to chance rather than you actually having a sixth sense.

Mind Reading

Believe it or not, some teens think that they can read minds! Well, not really, but they do think they can do it when it comes to something bad happening. *Mind Reading* is a style that plays in the collections of many teens. If you find yourself guessing what others think, then a Mind Reading style of anxious track is playing.

Say you are convinced that you know what your boyfriend is thinking. You might think this, "I'm sure he wants to break up with me. He's just avoiding me to let me down easy." Instead, remind yourself you are a student not a psychic.

Overgeneralization

When you take one small thing and use it to draw conclusions about lots of other things, then *Overgeneralization* style is playing in your mind's collection. It is like thinking you have ruined the cookie batter when you added a teaspoon too much of sugar. Or you might begin to feel anxious when you think that if you miss a single pass in football tryouts the coach will cut you from the team. If the Overgeneralization style plays loud and often, remind yourself that many factors contribute to what happens, not just one small thing. This can help you to keep the situation in perspective.

End of the World

When the *End of the World* style of anxious track is playing, you are convinced that terrible things are about to happen. You feel anxious most of the time because you are always expecting the next big disaster. Even when your parents tell you that your neighborhood is safe and secure, when you hear a scratching noise outside your bedroom window, you immediately think, "Someone's breaking in!" Sounds scary, but it might be helpful to know that there have been hundreds of End of the World prophecies and none has ever come true! Also, recall all the situations where you believed the worst would happen. Were you correct? If not, this can be a helpful reality check when this style is playing on repeat mode in your collection.

Should-y/Must-y Thinking

Shoulds, Musts, Shouldn'ts, Mustn'ts! *Should-y/Must-y* anxious tracks can beat you down! You think of all the things you should have done or must not do. After a while, you are less confident. You begin to wonder if you can do things, even easy things that you have already done before. Often the *shoulds* or *musts* set the bar too high for you, so you begin to worry a lot about whether you will be able to do it. You might think, "I must always get good grades," or "Everyone should like me at all times." You work constantly to meet these expectations and your life becomes stressful and not a lot of fun. You might not hang out with friends after school because you think, "I must get good grades." Your softball games are stressful because you think, "We must win." Your friends call you a perfectionist and you agree. Shoulds and musts (as well as the shoulds in sheep's clothing: have to, need to, ought to), put a lot of pressure on you and unnecessarily increase your anxiety. If Should-y/Must-y tracks are playing in your collection, change them into something that seems more doable and reasonable such as, "I would like to . . . ," "It would be nice if . . . ," and "I will do my best to . . ." These new tracks turn the heat down a notch or two. Try shooting for excellence not perfection. You will be surprised how far excellence will take you, and the ride will be a lot easier.

Mind Jumps

When your anxious mind jumps to conclusions before you have all the facts, the *Mind Jumps* style of anxious track may be playing. (You will learn more about these in Chapter 6, *Floating With Panic Attacks.*) Let's say you overhear friends making plans for the weekend and they stop talking when you walk up. Your anxious mind jumps to the conclusion, "They don't like me anymore. That's why they're not inviting me to hang out." You become anxious every time you talk to them and wonder what you have done to offend or upset them. If you have the Mind Jumps style in your collection, stop jumping and start building. When the situation occurs, try gathering facts and building a conclusion rather than jumping to a conclusion. Once you have gathered all the facts, what you think is happening is more likely to be what is truly happening.

As you read these common styles of anxious tracks, did any of them seem familiar? Perhaps many of these are in your anxious mind's collection or perhaps just a few. It may take a while to figure out the particular styles of anxious tracks that play most often in your collection. Sometimes a single track can have two styles, such as the thought "He thinks I'm ugly. He'll never ask me out." (This is an example of Mind Reading and Fortune Telling.) For many teens, their anxious tracks play automatically and very softly, so softly they might not be aware of what is playing. Knowing that your collection contains a lot of Mind Reading can help you change "She thinks I'm boring" to something more accurate. To figure out your style or styles of anxious tracks, review your A-B-C-D-E Logs. See if your tracks fit into a particular style or styles. Then, jot down the specific style corresponding with each thought in the D column on your Log.

CHANGING UNWANTED ANXIOUS TRACKS

Your anxious tracks or self-talk is a big part of why you are feeling anxious and afraid and why you avoid doing the things you want to do. As discussed, the A-B-C Model highlights how events (A) trigger self-talk (B), which in turn triggers anxiety and avoidance (C). It is the anxious self-talk that generates anxiety, not the event itself. Take a look at Clay's A-B-C-D-E Log. He learned that it was not the event of joining the basketball team (A) which elevated his anxiety and contributed to his performing well below his ability (C). But rather,

Clay's A-B-C-D-E Log

A	B	C
I joined the basketball team. This was what started my anxious mind going. Each time I thought about being on the team or was practicing with the team, my anxious tracks started.	**I'll mess up and get benched for the season.** This was the track that played the most in my anxious mind.	**My anxiety level is 7 out of 10.** I rated my anxiety pretty high since I was very anxious when listened to my self-talk. **I take and make easy shots. I don't take risks.** I found myself making easy shots and playing it safe. I didn't want to take any risks as I was sure this would result in my anxious tracks coming true.

A: activating event.
B: beliefs (anxious tracks).
C: consequences (feelings and actions).

it was his anxious track (B) that made him anxious and negatively affected his performance.

So, just like real music, you can learn to dub over and remix your anxious tracks to create new tracks that will calm your anxious mind. You probably know that sound engineers are the people who mix the music and lyrics that musicians produce. In the beginning, the sound engineer sorts through music and lyrics and identifies the tracks that are too loud, too soft, or have too much static. The sound engineer mixes, dubs over, and remixes the music and lyrics until the sound is smooth and harmonious. When this process is complete, the sound engineer makes the final cut and produces a song. These steps are similar to the steps you will take to learn to remix your anxious tracks.

Learning to change your anxious tracks will take some skill and practice. After all, these have been playing for a long time. It can help to use other tools you have learned in this book while you are remixing your anxious tracks, such as abdominal breathing, progressive muscle relaxation, visualization, getting some rest, or having a snack. Once you calm your anxious body, you will be better able to remix your anxious tracks using the Calm Mind tools described next.

Evidence For and Against (Fact vs. Opinion)

The first tool that can help you to remix your anxious tracks is *Evidence For and Against*. This tool involves learning the difference between facts and opinions. A fact can be determined to be true or false—correct or incorrect. An opinion, on the other hand, cannot be established as true or false—correct or incorrect. Sometimes your facts about an event are correct, but your opinions about the event are incorrect or blown out of proportion. For example, some teens will not do as well as other teens on a test. That is a fact. Thinking that you will fail the test, even after you have studied hard, is an opinion. To help determine if your anxious track is fact or opinion, create a Think Smart Checklist by following these steps:

1. At the top of the page, write down your anxious track.
2. Next, draw a line down the middle of the page to make two columns and a line across the top to form a big capital T. This is your T-chart.
3. At the top of the left column, write "Evidence for" and list all the evidence you can think of that makes your anxious track true or correct.

4. At the top of the right column, write "Evidence against" and, list all the evidence you can think of that makes your anxious track false or incorrect.

5. Next, ask yourself three questions: What is it that I think could happen? How likely is it that it would happen? What is more likely to happen? Record your thoughts beneath the two columns.

6. Now, what do you think? Does your original anxious track contain facts or opinions? If it seems to be an opinion, remix your track to include only the facts and develop a more accurate way of thinking about the situation.

7. At the bottom of your T-chart, write down your new remixed track.

This tool works well with most styles of anxious tracks. But if you have trouble thinking of much evidence that makes your track false or incorrect (evidence against), ask yourself what you would say to a friend if she wanted evidence to prove her anxious track was not true. Sometimes it is easier to see things clearly and objectively when we evaluate someone else's situation. If you are still having trouble getting the right remix, ask a parent or friend to help you evaluate both sides of your anxious track and to remix it.

Evaluating the evidence in your particular situation is exactly how a jury uses information presented by defendant's attorney and the plaintiff's attorney in arriving at a verdict. In evaluating the evidence, be careful that you do not confuse a feeling, which is similar to an opinion, with a fact. This is like saying to the judge, "Your honor, my client isn't guilty because I feel that he would never lie to you or the jury." It is also like when Ellie got an F on her math test even though she studied a lot. It would be correct for Ellie to say, "I messed up on the test." She made mistakes and did not get a passing grade. This is a fact. However, it would be incorrect for Ellie to say,

"I'm a terrible student and will never be able to learn math." This is an opinion. It is not correct and makes her feel overly anxious. Review Ellie's Checklist below, and see how she evaluated her anxious track and remixed it using the Evidence For and Against tool.

Ellie's Think Smart Checklist

My anxious track: I'm a terrible student and I'll fail this class.

Calm Mind Tool: Evidence For and Against

EVIDENCE FOR	EVIDENCE AGAINST
I failed my first quarter final. I receive tutoring every week.	I passed the second quarter final and got a 93% on the third quarter final. My tutor tells me I know the material well. Tutoring doesn't mean I'm a bad student. Tutoring helps me understand math and makes it easier to study for tests and do well.

Evidence review: As I reviewed my evidence I asked myself, "What is it that I think could happen?" At first I was thinking I was a terrible student, because I failed the first final and would, for sure, fail the class. But then I thought, "How likely is it that I would really fail?" and realized it wasn't very likely after all the studying I've done and the tutoring I've received. I realized it was more likely that I'd pass the class with at least a C or a B.

My remixed track: I got off to a rough start this year when I failed the first final, but I've improved since then. My tutor tells me I know the material well. Even if I do badly, I won't fail the class because my overall grade is a B.

Responsibility Pizza (Reattribution)

Another tool you can use to remix anxious tracks is the *Responsibility Pizza*. Sometimes anxious teens (and adults, too!) assume too much responsibility for things that are out of their control. These teens feel a lot of pressure to ensure everything goes well and that nothing bad happens. They believe that they are 100% responsible for the outcome in any given situation. As you can imagine, this can leave a teen feeling anxious and edgy a lot of the time. Fortunately, the Responsibility Pizza can help reattribute (or redistribute) the responsibility you feel to other factors. This will help you see that you alone are not responsible for the outcome. Taking only a share of the responsibility for something can help you to feel less guilty when it does not work out well. And keep in mind that the Responsibility Pizza works well with Should-y/Must-y tracks, although you can use it for any anxious track that has you feeling 100% responsible.

To make your Responsibility Pizza, think of an upsetting event that caused you to feel anxious. Now, complete the following steps to create your Think Smart Checklist:

1. List as many possible factors that contributed to the upsetting outcome (or will contribute to the outcome if the event has yet to occur).
2. Go down the list and estimate how much (in percent) each factor contributed (or will contribute) to the outcome.
3. Now, estimate how much (in percent) you believe you contributed to the outcome. Try to look at the situation objectively.
4. Review all the factors and their percentage of responsibility. Compare this to your percentage. How responsible are you compared to all the other factors? Be sure the total percentage adds up to 100%.
5. Using this new information, write out a more accurate track that accounts for all the factors and not just you.

To get an idea about how to remix your anxious track using the Responsibility Pizza, review Darcy's example below:

Darcy's Think Smart Checklist

My anxious track: My friends had a bad time, and it was all my fault.

Calm Mind Tool: Responsibility Pizza

CONTRIBUTING FACTORS	RESPONSIBILITY % (percentage)
Weather was bad.	20%
Mary was irritable.	15%
Movie was terrible.	30%
Schools has been stressful and we were distracted.	25%
I am responsible.	10%

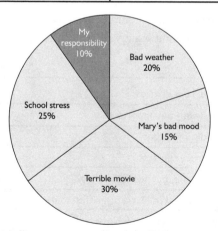

My remixed track: I'm only slightly responsible for my friends having a good time. Many other factors influence the quality of our time together.

Time Machine (De-catastrophizing)

The *Time Machine* is yet another useful Calm Mind tool. When End of the World anxious tracks are playing, you are making a small event into a monumental catastrophe. The Time Machine can help you feel less anxious by giving you a glimpse of the future. Time can provide some perspective on what feels, at the moment, like a disaster.

To use the Time Machine, consider a recent upsetting event and complete the following steps.

1. Write down the event and your anxious track.
2. On the next line, write down, "How important is this event and believing my anxious track at this moment?"
3. On the subsequent line, write down, "How important will this event and believing my anxious track be in an hour?"
4. On the subsequent line, write down, "How important will this event and believing my anxious track be in a day?"
5. Continue writing out these statements for the following time increments: a week, a month, a year, five years, and ten years.
6. Using the following scale, rate each statement.

1	Could not care less
2	Definitely not important
3	Mildly important
4	Almost important
5	Important, but not life altering
6	Important, but I have bigger fish to fry
7	Important, and I will take it seriously
8	Very important
9	Very, very important
10	My life and the welfare of my world as I know it depends on this

7. Review your ratings. Is there a difference between your ratings for the present, near future, and those far into the future? If you predict that this event and your anxious track will no longer matter or will matter much less in the future, use this new perspective to remix your anxious track. Use this template:

Even though _____

_____ (insert the event) makes me think

_____

_____

(insert your anxious track), it will become less important over time. In fact, after _____

_____

_____

(insert correct amount of time) it will be unimportant, and after _____

_____

(insert correct amount of time) I might not even remember the event.

Look at Min's example on page 66 to help you understand how she used the Time Machine to remix her anxious track.

Min's Think Smart Checklist

Event: I told Adam I love homework.

My anxious track: I can't believe I said that. He must think I'm a geek. I'll never get a boyfriend now.

Calm Mind Tool: Time Machine

STATEMENT	ANXIETY RATING (1–10)
How important is this event and believing my anxious track at this moment?	9
How important will this event and believing my anxious track be in an hour?	9
How important will this event and believing my anxious track be in a day?	7
How important will this event and believing my anxious track be in a week?	5
How important will this event and believing my anxious track be in a month?	3
How important will this event and believing my anxious track be in a year?	2–3
How important will this event and believing my anxious track be in 5 years?	1
How important will this event and believing my anxious track be in 10 years?	1

My remixed track: Even though telling Adam I love homework makes me think he thinks I'm a geek and that I'll never get a boyfriend, it will become less important over time. In fact, in a month it will be almost unimportant, and after a few years I'll probably have forgotten it!

Confidence Booster (How to Handle It)

The final Calm Mind tool is the *Confidence Booster*. When your anxious mind is playing End of the World tracks, you become convinced that the situation is unbearable and that you will not be able to handle it. However, many anxious teens underestimate their ability to cope. The Confidence Booster helps you handle your feared situation in case it happens, which increases your confidence in your ability to handle tough situations. Knowing that you can handle a situation can really slow down your Worry Wheel.

To use the Confidence Booster tool, complete the following steps.

1. Write the bad thing you worry will happen (this is the anxious track that you are going to remix).
2. Next, write all the ways you might handle the bad thing if it were to happen. Brainstorm as many ideas as you can. What do you think? Do you feel a little more confident that you will be able to handle the bad thing if it happens?
3. Finally, write a one- or two-liner (a real zinger) that reminds you that you can cope with the bad situation.

Check out how Bobbie used the Confidence Booster tool:

Bobbie's Think Smart Checklist

My anxious track: If the kids laugh at me, I'll feel so embarrassed I won't be able to handle it.

Calm Mind Tool: Confidence Booster

> How to handle it:
> Remember, I've felt embarrassed before and it always passes.
> I could talk to Gus and Stephanie and they would help me take it in stride.
> I could speak to my teacher and ask her to help me get through it. I don't want her to talk to the other kids—just tell me that it happens to every kid from time to time.

My remixed track: I can do many things to handle the embarrassment. I've handled embarrassment in the past, so I can do it this time, too.

THINKING SMART AND ACTING BRAVE

This chapter described how unhelpful anxious self-talk or tracks can cause you to feel anxious and avoid doing things that you might like to do. In addition, you learned some remix tools to change your anxious tracks and calm your anxious mind. In order to feel confident that you can use these tools to quickly calm your anxious mind, we recommend that you try to use the A-B-C-D-E Log and Calm Mind tools daily until you are able to remix unwanted anxious tracks. Here is how to become a remix expert. Begin by copying the A-B-C-D-E Log on the next page into a notebook, journal, or computer, and keep this in a place that you can get to it quickly, such as in your backpack or locker. When something stirs up your anxious mind, use a log and complete columns A, B, and C. Then as soon as you have the time, complete columns D and E, using a different Calm Mind tool for each new log entry. When you have used all of the tools several times, decide which tools work the best for you. You might like all of them equally, or there might be one tool that helps calm your anxious mind in most situations.

After several days of practice, you might notice that you are quickly catching unwanted anxious tracks and perhaps even completing an A-B-C-D-E Log in your mind. This means you are starting to "think smart" automatically. However, thinking smart is only one of the goals. The other goal is to change the way you act. As you learn to think smart, you will feel less anxious and perhaps ready to try some things that you may have been avoiding. We call this "acting brave," which we take up in the next chapter.

My A-B-C-D-E Log

A	B	C	D	E

A: activating events.
B: beliefs (anxious tracks).
C: consequences (feelings and actions).
D: disputing anxious tracks (Calm Mind tool).
E: effect of disputing anxious tracks (my remixed track).

CHAPTER 5

FACING FEARS ONE STEP AT A TIME

If you avoid certain things or situations, you may have a *phobia*. A phobia is a persistent and unreasonable fear of a specific object, activity, or situation that makes you want to avoid that object, activity, or situation. Ellie avoids a specific thing—spiders. Bobbie avoids going to parties or raising his hand to ask questions in class because he is afraid that kids will laugh at him or think that he is dumb. Min avoids touching doorknobs and hand railings on the stairs at school because she is afraid that she will catch some terrible disease. And Darcy avoids crowded rooms or elevators because she is afraid of enclosed spaces. Finally, there is Clay. Although he is not avoiding specific things or activities, he is worrying way too much about his grades, his athletic performance, and his future. Clay knows he has too much anxiety because he worries more than anyone he knows, and it takes up a lot of time each week. When his anxiety peaks, he starts thinking about avoiding or quitting, such as not going to college or not trying out for the basketball team.

Not everyone who is anxious avoids things, but if you do, facing it is the most effective way to overcome a phobia. You may think that you will never be able to face your fears. It may seem like an impossible task. But like many tasks, you can do it when you work on it one step at a time. In this chapter, you will learn how to put together your own Facing My Fear Plan that guides you through the whole process of facing those big and little fears that are taking up too much space in your life. We describe the importance of facing fears rather than avoiding them and then show you how to face your fears one step at a time.

LEARNING HOW TO BE AFRAID

Believe it or not, your mind is programmed to be afraid of some things, but not others. Since prehistoric times, humans have been afraid of certain things or situations that threaten survival, such as poisonous snakes, ferocious animals, heights, darkness (where predators hide), and closed-in places (where it might be difficult to escape from a predator). We call these *prepared fears,* meaning that we have an innate, hardwired tendency to fear these things. People are less likely to fear things that do not threaten their survival like kittens, lollipops, rainbows, or light bulbs.

However, we can learn to be afraid of anything, even those things that our minds were not prepared to fear. Learning to fear something can happen in three different ways—through personal experience, through observation, or through repeated warnings from others. Personal experience teaches us a lot. If we have a bad or terrifying experience with something, we might obviously become afraid. For example, we might become afraid of flying after we have a turbulent and scary plane ride. We also learn a lot when we observe others. So if we watch someone else being afraid of something, we might learn that, too. For example, if you watched one of your parents become very anxious or afraid while flying, you might become afraid of flying even if you never had a bad experience when flying. (Fears tend to run in families, which may be due to family members watching other family members being afraid of something.) Another way we learn to be afraid is that someone repeatedly warns us it is dangerous.

For example, a father who repeatedly tells his child that flying is dangerous can learn to fear flying.

Learning to be afraid really does happen. Take this example: you were taking a shortcut across a neighbor's yard one day and their big Labrador retriever runs up, barks, and snaps at you. He did not bite you, but he scared you. If you were very frightened, your mind learned and registered that "big Labrador retriever means fear." Since then, all you have to do is think about the neighbor's big Labrador retriever and you start to feel anxious. You do not like that feeling, so you avoid the neighbor's Lab, and you learn to control your anxiety by simply avoiding the dog. Soon you start to avoid all Labrador retrievers because they make you feel a little anxious, too. And then you avoid all dogs. Now you have a full-fledged dog phobia. Your anxious mind learned to be afraid of dogs, even safe, friendly ones. Regardless of the way you learned to become afraid, your fear of dogs is deep within you now. However, you can overcome even a deep fear, and the best way to do that is to face the fear one step at a time.

WHY FACE FEARS?

Continuing to avoid a situation or thing that frightens you keeps the phobia alive. You do not get the chance to challenge your anxious mind and unlearn what you learned to fear. Avoiding the situation or thing that frightens you may also limit your life by preventing you from doing the things you enjoy. Nothing works better in overcoming a fear than facing it—especially when you have a plan and do it a step at a time. Some kids figure this out themselves, like Donald Zinkoff in the book, *Loser* by Jerry Spinelli. Donald is a quirky but remarkable kid who happens to be deathly afraid of the furnace in his basement. One day, he decides to overcome his fear and develops a plan. Each day he plans to edge closer to the furnace, step by step, down the stairs, until he is face-to-face with his fear.

Even with a plan like Donald's, facing a fear is not easy. Facing your fear asks a lot of you but it gives back a lot, too. First, overcoming a fear feels good. It is a tremendous confidence booster. After you overcome your fear, we bet you will feel proud of yourself and, in general, more confident about many things, not just about overcoming the thing that frightened you. You may feel a little less anxious about tests or less anxious when you hang out with friends. Maybe you will feel a little less anxious about getting into college or landing your first job.

Second, you learn that fear goes away with time and, until it does, you can handle it. This lesson will pay off big time for you because most difficult things operate this way. At first, they are tough, but if you hang in there, things usually get easier.

Last, overcoming a fear gets people's attention in a good way. Your parents, brothers and sisters, friends, and teachers will see you in a new light. They will see you as a brave "can do" person, or someone who has a good attitude toward tough situations. That feels good, too. To get you into the "can do" mode, it might help to list all the reasons that you want to overcome your fear. Think about the long-term payoffs of facing your fear and not the short-term discomfort and write the reasons down.

I listed all the reasons I could think of about why I wanted to get over my fear of spiders, like "I want to go barefoot in the house" or "I don't want to have to sleep under a heavy blanket because I'm afraid that spiders will crawl on me." But the most important reason was that I wanted to go on the school trip to South America, where there are lots of spiders.

—Ellie, age 14

THINKING SMART AND ACTING BRAVE

As we introduced in Chapter 4 (*Thinking Smart*), your anxious mind plays a major role in keeping your fear powerful and in charge of your life. Typically, if you are afraid of a specific thing or situation, it is because you have learned to play one of two styles of anxious tracks in your mind. The first style is the Mind Jumps track. Remember, that is the one where your anxious mind jumps to scary conclusions before you have all the facts. The most common scary conclusion anxious teens make is that the bad thing is very likely to happen.

The second style of anxious track is the End of the World. This is where your anxious mind tells you that the bad thing is not just bad, but that it is horrible and dangerous, a real catastrophe. You believe that whatever happens is too big to handle, and you will never survive.

Later in this chapter, you will learn how to build your Facing My Fear Plan. This plan will have several pieces, including a Think Smart Checklist and a Fear Ladder. First, go back and review the Calm Mind tools for remixing your anxious tracks that you learned in Chapter 4 to help build your own Think Smart Checklist at the end of this section. The tool that works well to remix your Mind Jumps track is the Evidence For and Against tool. This tool works by reminding you that there is a difference between facts and opinions. Remember, facts are pieces of evidence about an event. Facts can be determined to be true or false—correct or incorrect. Opinions, on the other hand, are the way we see things and cannot be established as true or false—correct or incorrect. For example, Darcy believes that she will suffocate if she is stuck in an elevator between floors. Fortunately, Darcy was able to remix her Mind Jumps track by using the Evidence For and Against tool.

Darcy's Think Smart Checklist

My anxious track: I'll suffocate if the elevator is stuck.

Calm Mind Tool: Evidence For and Against

EVIDENCE FOR	EVIDENCE AGAINST
When it's crowded in the elevator, I feel like I can't catch my breath.	Elevators are not airtight. If people could suffocate in an elevator, there probably would be some warning about this. I have asked some of my friends whether they thought it likely that you could suffocate in an elevator, and they all said, "No way." If people suffocated in elevators, the government would either outlaw elevators or put some kind of breathing mask in them. Elevators are still legal, and I have not seen any breathing masks. When the elevator is crowded, the air inside can get warm, which makes me feel like I am suffocating. But feeling like I am not getting enough air does not mean I am suffocating. It probably means I am anxious!

My remixed track: Elevators are not airtight so air is always circulating inside. When I'm anxious, I feel like I'm suffocating, but really, I'm just anxious. No one has ever suffocated in an elevator. I think I would hear about that!

Another tool that can help you remix End of the World tracks involves developing a Confidence Booster. Remember, the idea here is to focus on how you would handle the situation rather than telling yourself that you cannot or that the situation is unbearable or horrible. As you read in Chapter 4, Bobbie's anxious mind is playing an End of the World track. He is convinced that all the kids in his class will laugh at him if he answers a question incorrectly. Although Bobbie realizes that it is more likely that just one or two kids will laugh at him, he also would like to believe that he could handle it if that happens. He remixed his anxious track with a Confidence Booster and came up with this: "I can do many things to handle the embarrassment. I've handled embarrassment in the past, so I can do it this time, too."

To complete your Think Smart Checklist at the end of the chapter, simply write out your anxious track. In the left column, write your Calm Mind tool, followed by your new, remixed track in the right hand column. You may notice that you use the Evidence For and Against and Confidence Booster tools for many of your anxious tracks in preparation to face a specific fear. However, the Responsibility Pizza and Time Machine tools can also be effective in remixing anxious tracks.

BUILDING YOUR FEAR LADDER

A large part of your Facing My Fear Plan is your *Fear Ladder*. Just as it says, your Fear Ladder is a scale of situations that make you anxious. The bottom rungs of the ladder make you mildly anxious while the top ones make you most anxious. Your plan will help you face your fear slowly as you climb the ladder, step by step. Facing your fear directly like this works best for teens who are avoiding social situations, such as speaking in public, attending parties, using public restrooms, or taking tests. It works great for overcoming your fear of certain places, too. If you have panic disorder and agoraphobia, you might avoid going into shopping malls, restaurants, buses, or subways. If you are avoiding certain things like dogs, needles, insects, or germs, facing your fears one step at a time also will help.

Break Down Your Fear

In order to create a ladder of fear-busting steps, begin by breaking the fear down. First, think about various ways you can change the situation to make it more or less scary. For example, how close you are to the thing or situation might affect how anxious you feel. If you are afraid of heights, standing 2 feet away from a window in a tall building might be scarier than standing 5 feet away from the edge, or standing on the first rung of a ladder might be scarier than standing on the second rung. Another way to adjust how anxious you feel is to think about how much time you would stay in the situation. For example, if you are afraid of enclosed spaces, standing in a closet for 2 minutes might be easier than standing in the closet for 10 minutes. Sometimes, the size of something affects how scared you feel. A large dog may be scarier than a small dog, or a large needle may be scarier than a small one.

In addition to breaking down your fear, it is important to describe each step on the ladder clearly and specifically. If you cannot clearly describe what you are going to do, you might not be able to do it. The more specific you make the description, the less anxious and more confident you will feel in being able to do the step. Writing out "Look at a dog that is being held by his leash from 6 feet away" is clearer and more specific than "Look at a dog." That description could be a very scary step because you do not know if that means you look at the dog that is across a parking lot from you or if it means you look at the dog as it sits on your lap. When Ellie built her ladder, she broke down her fear into manageable steps and rated each step (0 = no anxiety or fear, 10 = maximum anxiety or fear).

When you are building your Fear Ladder, try to have at least 8–12 steps on your Fear Ladder. Although, your ladder may have as many as 20, this can feel somewhat overwhelming to tackle.

Ellie's Fear Ladder

Facing My Fear of Spiders

SITUATION	FEAR RATING (0–10)
Letting a daddy longlegs crawl on my shoulder.	10
Letting a daddy longlegs crawl up my arm.	9
Holding a daddy longlegs on the palm of my hand for as long as I can.	8.5
Touching a daddy longlegs quickly.	7
Touching a daddy longlegs through the glass of the sealed jar that my mom is holding.	6
Looking at a real daddy longlegs in a sealed jar that my mom is holding.	5.5
Watching a YouTube video clip of a daddy longlegs crawling about.	5
Holding a picture of a daddy longlegs while I touch the picture of the head of the daddy longlegs.	4
Touching a picture of a daddy longlegs while my mom holds the picture.	3
Looking at the head of a daddy longlegs while my mom holds the picture.	2
Looking at a picture of a daddy longlegs while my mom holds the picture.	1

Similarly, fewer than eight steps may make your Fear Ladder more difficult because it may not have enough lower anxiety steps.

Also, build a ladder that has a situation on every step with lower steps (mildly anxious) gradually building to top steps (most anxious). If the first Fear Ladder you build only has the top steps filled with situations, you may have trouble climbing it because you will have to jump to the top right away. The best thing about the process of facing your fear in steps is that you start on the lower steps to build your confidence. These lower steps are not too scary, and because of that, you are much more likely to succeed.

When you are working on your Fear Ladder, remember the difference between an *actual danger* and a *perceived danger* (which is when we believe that something is dangerous when it is not). You will want to work on perceived dangers. For example, Ellie is going to face her fear of spiders by facing daddy longlegs, which are safe. Ellie is not going to become less fearful of black widow spiders, which are dangerous. Min is going to face her fear of getting sick by touching the kitchen counter, which is dirty but safe because her family touches the doorknob and is fine. Similarly, a teen who wants to overcome his fear of dogs would face a dog that he knows is friendly and never bites, rather than a dog that he does not know or a dog that bites from time to time.

To create your own Fear Ladder, take the following steps:

1. Determine what fear you would like to face and write that down.
2. Make certain that what you are planning to face is safe. (Ask a friend or your parents whether they think the situation is safe. Would they do this?)
3. List about 8–12 situations that relate to your fear. Write these into the Situation and Step column. Try to cover all the steps from extremely scary and difficult to mildly scary and not so

difficult to face, with the scariest situation at the top and the least scary at the bottom.

4. Next, in the Fear Rating column, rate how frightened you would feel (0 = no anxiety or fear, 10 = maximum anxiety or fear).

Imagine Your Fear

Ellie created a Fear Ladder for a real-life situation. You can build a Fear Ladder for imagined situations, too. You might be thinking, "What's the point? Imagining something that frightens me isn't going to make me very anxious." Exactly. That is one of the reasons this way of facing your fear can help. Imagining the thing or situation that frightens you is a great way to warm up to the scarier way of facing your fear—by doing it. For some teens, imagining a fear helps them so much that they do not need to spend a lot of time facing the fear directly. In addition, many times, what you imagine is far scarier than the real thing.

Imagining it can also decrease the anxiety you feel before you even see the thing or enter a situation that frightens you. Much of the fear you have about flying, riding in an elevator, or spiders comes from your thoughts about the thing or situation and what you imagine might happen. We call this *anticipatory anxiety*. Many teens worry for hours or days before they make a speech or go to the dentist. Imagining it can lower your anxiety and worry about these kinds of things.

The last reason to face your fear by imagining it is that imaging it may be the only way to get you into the situation. Some teens are afraid of things and situations that you cannot face directly or that would not be safe to face directly. For example, the scariest thing about spiders for Ellie was that a spider would bite her and she would feel a horrible pain that would last forever. To overcome this part of her fear by doing it, Ellie would have to let a spider actually bite her. This is not safe, and it is not necessary because Ellie can imagine this. Similarly, Bobbie can imagine all the kids in his class laughing at him. He does not have to do this in reality because, really, what is the point? In order to get all the kids to laugh at him, Bobbie would probably have to do something ridiculous, which would likely get him in a ton of trouble with his teacher. This is not dangerous, but it is not necessary, either. In addition, teens can face some situations directly but not often enough to overcome their fear. Flying is a good example of this. Most teens cannot fly often enough to overcome their fear of flying completely without imagining it.

You can build this *imagine-it* Fear Ladder in the same way as the *doing-it* Fear Ladder by following the steps in page 80. Or you can use cards or slips of paper to write how you might deal with the situation.

Begin with imagined situations that cause you little or low anxiety, all the way up to imagined situations that cause you higher or extreme anxiety. When you have created these scenes in your head, the next step is to write them out on paper and give them a fear rating. Writing out each imagined situation is a little bit like writing a movie script, where you elaborate in detail each part of the scene. Using all five senses can help bring your imagined situation into focus.

I used index cards when I built my Fear Ladder. On each card, I wrote a way to face my fear of crowded rooms, and then arranged the cards from least scary to most scary and numbered them with a fear number of 0 to 10. All this actually made me feel less afraid of going to the mall. I could see that I had a plan to face my fears.

—Darcy, age 17

The final step is to record these scenes. You can write it down and read it to yourself or have someone read it to you, or you can use an old-fashioned tape player or digital voice recorder describing the scene. Here is what Bobbie recorded. He gave this a fear number of 8.

I'm sitting in math class listening to the teacher. It's a warm day, and I am sweating slightly. I can hear the sound of lawn mowers in the distance, and I can smell cut grass. The teacher asks a question, and I think I know the answer, although I'm not sure. I decide to tell her what I think and raise my hand. As I do, kids start to laugh. I haven't even said anything, and I can hear them laughing. I begin to feel nervous. I start to sweat more. My mouth is dry, and I'm finding it difficult to breathe. I drop my hand and slouch down. I can't look at the other kids. I hear the teacher telling them to be quiet, but they keep laughing. I feel terrible. I have never felt this embarrassed in my life, but I can't leave. I'm frozen in my seat, waiting for it to pass, but the kids keep laughing and laughing—on and on.

DEVELOPING YOUR FACING MY FEAR PLAN

Now it is time to put together all the pieces of your Facing My Fear Plan. The plan has three parts. The first part is the situation you plan to face. This comes from your Fear Ladder, and you will write that on the line next to "The fear I face today," along with the date. Next, you will write your remixed track that you wrote out on your Think Smart Checklist. Then finally, there is a *Fear Thermometer*—we will get to that soon—to monitor your anxiety level when you are facing your fear by doing it or imagining it.

FACING YOUR FEAR

Once you have created your Facing My Fear Plan, you are ready for the hardest part—facing your fear. You will begin on the lowest step of your Fear Ladder, facing the situation that creates the least anxiety. It is important to have a way to monitor your anxiety so that you can see that your anxiety goes down over time. You will use a Fear Thermometer to record how anxious you are each time you face your fear, where 0 is cool and calm and 10 is the most anxious or frightened you can imagine being. You will circle the number on the Fear Thermometer that corresponds to the highest your anxiety reached each time you faced your fear. Your plan might mean you face the fear you listed on "The fear I face today" line several times during that day.

Before you begin facing your fear, read your Think Smart Checklist. Repeat these phrases to yourself several times before you begin. Even better, ask your mom or dad (or a good friend) to practice with you for a few minutes before you face your fear. You can have fun with it, with you playing the part of your calm mind and speaking your remixed tracks and having your coach play your anxious mind and speaking your anxious tracks. Do this back and forth until you are confident you have it down pat and you feel ready to begin.

Although you can expect to feel a mild to medium level of anxiety as you begin to face your fears, some teens notice a spike in their anxiety that makes it hard to get started. If this happens to you, consider using other coping tools outlined in this book such as taking some calm deep breaths or visualizing a peaceful scene in your mind. Alternatively, review your Fear Ladder. Perhaps you decided to begin on a step midway up your ladder, thinking it would be easy, when in fact it is harder than you expected. Remember, it is important to start near the bottom of your ladder and climb up to the top.

Now, face your fear. When you begin to face your fear, it is important that you stay in the situation and record your Fear Thermometer reading every 2 to 5 minutes. For example, Ellie began to face her fear by looking through a book about spiders. She decided to do a Fear Thermometer every time she went through the book. When she looked at a picture, she recorded her fear on the Fear Thermometer every 2 minutes until her fear was 0 or 1. That took her about 30 minutes. But if it takes you a little longer, keep going. The most important thing for you is to stay with it until your anxiety goes down to 0 or 1. Now take a look at Clay's Fear Plan on page 89 to see how he put it all together.

If you want to see the Facing My Fear Plans for the other teens, check out the Additional Resources section at the end of the book. However, your Plan will probably look different because no two teens are the same, and no two fears are the same, either. If you are going to face your fear, we want to make certain you get the most out of every try. We want you to succeed every time.

GETTING THE MOST OUT OF EVERY TRY

You may think you have already tried facing your fears and that it did not work. Bobbie thought that, too, at first: "Hey, facing my fear didn't work for me. My mom and dad made me go to the big family holiday party. I had to stay there, but I was anxious and miserable the whole time." In this example, Bobbie's mom and dad forced him to go to the holiday party. People forcing you to face your fear is not the same as you planning to do it, starting on a low step of your ladder and practicing again and again until you can do it easily with little or no anxiety. For that reason, if you are willing to take a chance and face your fear, it is important that you do it in a way that pays off. When facing your fear, follow these six rules to get the most out of every try:

- Do it in steps.
- Do it until the fear is gone.
- Do it often.

- Do it fully.
- Do it smart.
- Do it with help.

DO IT IN STEPS. The best way to succeed each time is to break down your fear into steps. When you break your fear into steps on your Fear Ladder, you will feel less anxious because you are getting the big picture. You may think that when you have a phobia, your fear works like a light switch—on when you are anxious and off when you are not. The truth about fear is that it is more like a dimmer switch. There are many little steps along the way from feeling a little anxious to feeling terrified. Knowing that you can take small steps will make facing a fear less scary because you will feel more confident and that you can do each step along the way.

DO IT UNTIL THE FEAR IS GONE. Hang out with the fear and stay in the situation until your fear decreases. Usually, that takes less than 60 minutes, but sometimes it may take longer. It is important that you face your fear long enough that you learn that whatever you worry about rarely or never happens and that you can handle your anxiety for as long as it takes. Check your fear level every couple of minutes. When your fear is at 0 or 1 you can stop, but do not stop before that.

DO IT OFTEN. Practice facing your fear at least four or five times a week and take at least one day off each week to reward yourself for your efforts. Each time you practice, start where you left off before you go to the next step. This is your warm-up step. Remember, though, when you do your warm-up, you may feel a little more anxious than the day before. That is okay. Just hang out on that step until the anxiety goes away, and then you are ready to try your next step.

Do It Fully. Facing a fear is not fun. You can expect to feel anxious, and when you do, you know that you are on the right track to overcoming your fear. Because you are feeling anxious, you might be tempted to fight the feeling or do things to lessen your anxiety a bit. To get the most out of each try, hang out with the anxiety rather than trying to push it away. When you practice, do not distract yourself from your anxious feelings or do little things to lessen your fear (rubbing your hands on your pants to clean them if you are trying not to wash, looking at your feet when you are speaking to someone rather than looking him in the eye). Fully accept the risk, no matter how small.

Do It Smart. Before each practice, go over your Think Smart Checklist. This reminds your anxious mind to think smart. Then watch what really happens rather than what your anxious mind fears will happen. This will help your anxious mind unlearn what it fears.

Do It With Help. Last, you may want to ask someone to coach you as you face your fear. Pick someone with whom you feel comfortable and who will not push you to do more than the step you are ready to work on. A little support and encouragement when you are feeling anxious and unsure will help a lot. Remember to reward yourself after each practice. Make a list of rewards and talk these over with your parents (downloading a song, staying over at friend's house, having ice cream out with the family). They may have some ideas, too. Reward yourself only when you do what you plan. That is the best way to keep on track.

FINDING COURAGE

That is it. You are ready to start facing your own fears now. However, before you get started, we want to say something about courage. Some teens believe that courage is about not feeling scared. This

Clay's Facing My Fear Plan

Today's date: July 15

The fear I face today: Being able to study 30 minutes less for my math test.

My anxious track: I'll fail my math test.

Think Smart Checklist

CALM MIND TOOL	REMIXED TRACK
Evidence For and Against	I'm good in math and study more than is necessary. Studying 30 minutes less probably won't make any difference in my grade. Even if I don't do well on this math test, it's not the end of the world.
Confidence Booster	If I fail my math test because I studied a little less, I can handle that. I can always ask the teacher for some extra credit. I don't have to get an A on every test to feel good.

My remixed track: I always pass my math test, regardless of how much I study. And I don't have to get an A on every test to feel good about myself.

Fear Ladder

SITUATION AND STEP	FEAR RATING (0–10)
Study 30 minutes less than usual for a math test.	8
Study 25 minutes less than usual for a math test.	7
Study 20 minutes less than usual for a math test.	6
Study 15 minutes less than usual for a math test.	5
Study 10 minutes less than usual for a math test.	4
Study 8 minutes less than usual for a math test.	3
Study 5 minutes less than usual for a math test.	2
Study 3 minutes less than usual for a math test.	1

Clay's Fear Thermometer

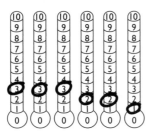

My Facing My Fear Plan

Today's date: _____

The fear I face today: _____

My anxious track: _____

Think Smart Checklist

CALM MIND TOOL	REMIXED TRACK

My remixed track: _____

_____

_____

_____

(continued)

My Facing My Fear Plan *(continued)*

Fear Ladder

SITUATION AND STEP	FEAR RATING (0–10)

My Fear Thermometer

CHAPTER 6

FLOATING WITH PANIC ATTACKS

You may know about riptides or rip currents. These are strong currents (1 to 5 miles per hour) near the shore and near the surface of the water. Rip currents pull you out to sea. People do not usually drown in a rip current if they do not try to fight it by swimming directly toward shore. If you do try to fight it, you will tire because a rip current is much stronger than you are. Once you are exhausted, you sink (you are not pulled) under the water. End of story.

So if fighting a rip current is not the smart thing to do, what is? Lifeguards would tell you to relax when a rip current catches you because you can keep yourself afloat easily—you dog paddle for a while, you do the backstroke for a while, you tread water for a while—and you wait. A rip current does not pull you under (it pulls you out for a bit), so you are safe so long as you float. Soon the current will die out and you are free to swim into shore.

Same thing with panic. While we do not want you to fight your panic, we do not want you to ignore it and do nothing, either. The best thing to do is float. The goal of this chapter is for you to learn how to detect when a panic attack is building and what to do about it. We will describe the typical features that contribute to the experience of panic and present strategies to help teens float with panic and get through panic attacks.

DEFINING FEAR AND PANIC

People have fear. Animals have fear. You have it, too. *Fear* is just a natural response to danger. You might have learned about the *fight-or-flight response* in a science class, but all it means is that you are instantaneously and instinctually prepared to fight or run away from a life-threatening situation. Your heart beats faster, you become extra alert, and your muscles are at the ready. You are prepared for action. Fear protects animals in the wild when they face a predator, and it makes it possible for you to escape danger if you can, or to defend yourself if you must. If you were walking down the sidewalk and you saw someone on a bicycle heading straight at you, you would jump out of the way. In this situation, your fear protects you from a nasty bump or worse. However, when you have a fear reaction but there is not a real danger or life-threatening situation around, that is called panic.

Panic or a *panic attack* is a sudden rush of fear that seems to come from nowhere, but the feelings are very real. Basically, a panic attack is a fear response that has misfired. During a panic attack, your heart can beat very fast and you can sweat, feel dizzy, and have trouble breathing. Sometimes you might feel like you are choking or you might shake and tremble. At the same time as your body feels anxious, your mind sounds the alarm, too. You might think you are going crazy, dying, or that you will "lose it" and run around, screaming at the top of your lungs. Most of all, you want to get away—out of the classroom, out of the elevator, off the plane. Your Anxious Action is to escape. But why? Why do you feel panic? Why does your mind sound the alarm in the first place?

JUMPING TO PANIC

When you have panic, your anxious mind and body are sounding the alarm that something bad or dangerous is happening to you. Except that it is not. Panic attacks are not even a little bit dangerous.

More surprising still, panic attacks are an entirely natural reaction that simply occurs at the wrong time or in the wrong situation. Because there is no real danger when you are having these intense bodily fear sensations, your mind will invent or jump to reasons that make sense to your anxious mind. We call these your *Mind Jumps to Panic*. These are actually anxious tracks playing when you are in panic mode (Remember the A-B-C Model in Chapter 4?). There are six common kinds of anxious tracks that that can cause teens to jump to panic.

- I'm having a heart attack.
- I'm going to faint or pass out.
- I'm going to stop breathing and suffocate.
- I'm going to fall or not be able to walk.
- I'm going crazy.
- I'm losing control.

I'M HAVING A HEART ATTACK. When you have a panic attack, your heart begins to beat very fast. If you were sprinting down the track—no problem—you would think, "Of course my heart is beating really fast, I'm running hard." Perhaps you would not even notice. However, when your heart is beating very fast, and you cannot think of a good reason why that is happening, your mind might jump to the thought "I'm having a heart attack" or "I'm to going to die."

Although it is scary when your heart beats very fast, this is not dangerous—particularly if you are healthy. Healthy hearts can beat very fast for many hours without anything bad happening. During a panic attack, you might feel your heart miss or add a beat or two, or you might feel some pain in the left-upper part of your chest, which passes quickly. Furthermore, none of these things gets worse when you move quickly or exert yourself. That is different if you are having a heart attack. During a real heart attack, most people feel a crushing pain in the center of the chest that gets worse when they exert themselves, and it does not go away. During a real heart attack, a person's heart might race or pound, but this usually happens after the pain starts. This is very different from a panic attack. That is why you want to move around. Your heart is pounding and pumping fast because your body is preparing you to fight or run away.

I'll never forget my first panic attack. I was watching TV in my room when it hit me. I started to sweat and my heart was beating really fast. I thought I was having a heart attack. I screamed for my mom and dad and they called 911. I spent the next four hours in the ER. The doctors hooked me up to a bunch of machines and checked my heart again and again. When they said I was fine, I didn't believe them. This was last year, and now I can look back and see how silly I was acting, but when it happened, I was really scared. I thought for sure I was dying.

—Darcy, age 17

I'M GOING TO FAINT OR PASS OUT. Some teens feel light-headed or dizzy when they have a panic attack. If you felt dizzy when you stood up very fast, your mind would think, "Whoa, I guess I stood up too quickly." But when this happens during a panic attack, your mind might jump to the thought "I'm going to faint" or "I'm going to pass out."

You feel dizzy because a little less blood is going to your brain, and instead, it is going to your muscles to prepare you to fight or run away. Although you might feel like you are going to faint, it is unlikely this would happen. Why? Because you are afraid, and because you are afraid, your heart is pumping harder than usual, which increases your blood pressure. We tend to faint when our blood pressure drops suddenly, and that is not happening. Therefore, as long as your heart is pounding as it is, you will not faint. This is a good example of how sophisticated our bodies are. (There are, of course, exceptions to every rule, so some teens might faint. For instance, a teen who has a blood phobia might faint at the sight of blood.)

I'M GOING TO STOP BREATHING AND SUFFOCATE. Some teens feel like they are having trouble breathing when they have a panic attack. The teen reports that his chest feels tight and heavy. He gasps to get more and more air into his lungs. When you become anxious, your neck and chest muscles, like the rest of your muscles, are tense and tight, which makes it a little harder to breathe. As you have more trouble breathing, your mind jumps to the thought "I'm going to stop breathing, and I'll suffocate."

This just does not make sense. You do not stop breathing when you have a panic attack. Your brain is smarter than that. Your brain has built-in reflexes that take care of you. If you stopped breathing, your brain would force you to breathe the way it forces you to breathe if you hold your breath too long. During a panic attack, you are getting plenty of oxygen. Even if you did pass out—not that it is likely—you would immediately start breathing and wake up. Now, we are not saying that feeling as if you are choking or having trouble breathing is comfortable, because it is not. However, it is not dangerous.

I'M GOING TO FALL OR NOT BE ABLE TO WALK. At times, during a panic attack, your legs may shake or tremble, or you may feel "weak in the knees" and have trouble walking. When this happens, your anxious mind might jump to the thought "I'm going to fall" or "I won't be able to walk." This can frighten you even more if you worry that if you fall or have trouble walking, people will think you are weird and you will embarrass yourself. Again, your anxious mind has jumped to a scary thought, but your legs are strong, and they will carry you when and where you want to go. During a panic attack, the blood vessels in your legs can dilate a bit, which causes blood to accumulate in your leg muscles and not fully circulate. This is not dangerous but it does make it feel like your legs are weak and heavy. The trembling and weakness will pass. If you have had several panic attacks, you probably know this. Did you fall down? No. Think about this for a minute. A panic attack is the fear response gone awry, right? If there is a real danger, your body will work just the way it was designed to work—to get you out of danger quickly. If our legs failed us every time we were frightened, our ancestors would not have survived very long in a world of mastodons and saber-toothed cats!

I'M GOING CRAZY. Some teens feel disoriented or out of touch with their surroundings during a panic attack. They report that they feel strange or weird, and they do not understand why. We admit that when you have a panic attack, you can have some rather strange feelings, and if you have never felt this way before, your mind can jump to the thought "I'm going crazy."

During a panic attack, a little less blood is flowing to your brain because your body has decided it needs to direct the blood to other parts of your body, like the big muscles you would use to defend yourself or run away from danger. This can cause you to feel strange or out of it, but that does not mean that you are going crazy, no matter how weird or strange you might feel. In fact, no one really goes "crazy" all of a sudden. Mental disorders tend to develop slowly over many years and panic attacks do not cause them. As scary as it is, a panic attack has never caused a teen to go crazy. Not ever!

I'm Losing Control. During a panic attack, you are feeling some pretty intense physical sensations and it is easy to imagine that you are losing control of yourself. In part, that is because your body feels so out of control. However, when your mind jumps to the thought "I'm losing it," what does that really mean? Some teens think it means that they are going to do something like run around and scream at the top of their lungs in terror. Other teens think it means that they will say or do something embarrassing. Maybe not as dramatic as running around and screaming, but embarrassing nonetheless.

If during a panic attack you feel like you want to jump up and run away, that does not mean you are losing control. It means that your mind and body have focused on one thing—getting you away from danger. This is exactly what you would want your mind and body to do if there were a real danger. Furthermore, running away from danger is not the same as losing control. Teens never really lose control. They just leave the situation if they can.

Now, what are your Mind Jumps to Panic? Take a few minutes to think about your anxious tracks that keep pushing you to panic.

BUILDING THE PANIC WAVE

Although many teens believe panic attacks come out of nowhere, they really build slowly like a wave. As you have learned, anxious tracks can cause the *Panic Wave* to crest. However, just like the wind, the tide, and the depth of the water below, other things contribute to how fast and to how strong a real wave builds and crests, the same is true for a Panic Wave. Look at the diagram on page 102. Let's start with your body, which plays an important role in your Panic Wave. If your schoolwork, your friends, or your family has been stressing you out for a while, your body is likely becoming more and more tense. A tense body can be the first signal that your Panic Wave is building. In

The Panic Wave

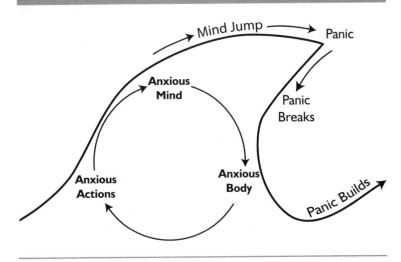

addition, it is not unusual for a routine body sensation to jump-start your anxious tracks. That is because when your mind jumps to panic, it always starts with something about your body that seems different or worrisome. Let's say you were having trouble breathing because you had a cold or your allergies were acting up. Your mind might jump from your stuffy nose to the scary assumption that you are suffocating. In addition, as you worry about having a panic attack, your body becomes more and more tense and stressed. This build-up of tension, whether because of a current stressor or worry about having a panic attack, contributes to the Panic Wave slowly building over hours, days, or even weeks.

Another factor that contributes to your Panic Wave building is your attention—that is, what you pay attention to when you are feeling tense or anxious about having a panic attack. As you have learned, when you think that danger may be around the corner, you begin to look for that danger. In the case of panic, because your mind jumps to something being wrong with your body, you tend to pay attention to any little change in your body. Even when you are studying or shooting baskets, a part of your anxious mind is scanning your body for the danger signs: "Am I breathing normally, or am I having trouble catching my breath?" "Is my heart beating okay, or is it jumping or missing beats?" Your attention pushes the Panic Wave ahead, because you are constantly looking for the danger and, typically, you find something that is not quite right, even if it is not dangerous.

As you learned earlier in this chapter, your anxious mind plays an important role in the building Panic Wave, too. Your anxious mind is always worrying a bit about whether your body is in control or out of control or whether the physical sensations are just a little different from the way they felt a moment ago, which might mean you are headed toward another panic attack. Your anxious mind is always worrying about your body and worrying about whether another panic attack is on the way. As you might guess, this worry causes your body to become even more tense and anxious. Soon, you begin to notice some physical sensation that is likely due to your body being tense or stressed. You think that something is wrong. Your anxious mind then jumps to panic ("I'm having a heart

Panic Wave Cycle

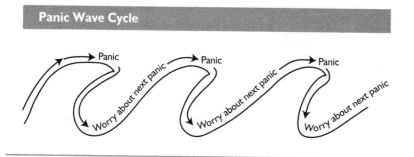

attack."). The Mind Jump to Panic happens in a second. The Panic Wave, however, can build over many hours or days.

FIGHTING THE PANIC WAVE (DON'T!)

As we have discussed, when your anxious mind jumps to panic, you might think that you are going crazy, that you are going to stop breathing and die, or that other dangerous things are about to happen. Of course, this is frightening, and you will want to get away from the danger as soon as possible. Sometimes you cannot and that is when you will begin to fight the panic that is building. You can try to push the panic away, but unlike real danger, like a dog that is trying to bite you, you cannot get away from your anxious mind and body. No matter what you do or where you go, there you are, and there is your panic.

It is very important to understand that trying to fight the initial feelings of panic is 90% of the problem. Fighting the beginnings of the Panic Wave—although even that is not a guarantee that you will panic—increases the likelihood you will panic. That is because it is not possible to fight panic. It is too strong. When you try to push down or fight something that cannot be pushed down or pushed away, you will fail, and as you fail, you will feel more and more out of control until—boom—the wave peaks and you panic.

Therefore, it is very important that you not fight the beginnings of the Panic Wave by trying to make it go away. Instead, we want you to learn to float. As described in the opening of this chapter, it might help you to think about your panic like a riptide, and fighting a rip current is not the smart thing to do. It is best to keep yourself afloat while you wait for the Panic Wave to die out. But before we teach you how to float on your Panic Wave, you will need to know when it is coming so you can catch it. Look at this Anxiety Scale, paying particular attention to those early panic stages.

Anxiety Scale

STAGE 0 ANXIETY (relaxing)	STAGE 1 ANXIETY (slight anxiety)	STAGE 2 ANXIETY (mild anxiety)	STAGE 3 ANXIETY (moderate anxiety)	STAGE 4 ANXIETY (marked anxiety)	STAGE 5 ANXIETY (early panic)	STAGE 6 ANXIETY (moderate panic attack)	STAGE 7 ANXIETY (major panic attack)
Calm, feeling undistracted, and at peace	Feeling slightly nervous, a passing twinge of anxiety	Definitely feeling nervous, butterflies in your stomach, feeling tense and a bit jumpy	Feeling uncomfortable but still in control, heart is beating faster, breathing faster, palms or upper lip feels sweaty	Feeling uncomfortable or "spacey," heart is beating very fast, worried about maintaining control, tense and antsy	Heart pounding or beating irregularly, feeling dizzy or "out of it," definitely afraid of "losing it," feeling the urge to escape or leave the situation	Heart beating strongly, having trouble breathing, feeling confused, feeling like you're only partly present, feeling like you're losing control	Everything in Stage 6 but ramped up, feeling terrified like you're going crazy or dying, looking for a way to get out of the situation

Note. Adapted with permission by New Harbinger Publications, Inc. *The Anxiety & Phobia Workbook, 4th Edition* by Edmund J. Bourne. www.newharbinger.com

CATCHING YOUR PANIC WAVE

Before you can float on a Panic Wave, you have to know when to catch it. Just like catching a wave when you are surfing, you have to get a little ahead of your Panic Wave. Catching the Panic Wave means knowing where you are on the Anxiety Scale. Different teens have different signs that their Panic Wave is building but most teens feel something. One teen might feel queasy or like she is going to throw up when she feels very anxious. As she becomes more anxious, she might begin to feel like she is having trouble breathing. She may believe she is losing control or that she is about to die because she cannot breathe. Other teens may begin to feel a little dizzy or notice that they are breathing faster or deeper or that their heart is beating faster. What feelings happen to you? If it is hard to think about all of your signs right away, try asking a parent or psychotherapist for help. If you are really stuck, pay attention the next time you have a panic attack and then jot down your signs.

FLOATING ON YOUR PANIC WAVE

When the first physical signs of your Panic Wave start to appear (Stage 4 or below), it is time to float. In addition to the feelings and sensations you are having, you will notice that your mind is most certainly jumping. The first thing you will need to do is to remix those anxious tracks into Jump Back tracks.

Jump Backs

Jump Backs are a kind of self-talk that cancels Mind Jumps to Panic. Jump Backs work because they accurately interpret what is going on and make sense of the feelings and sensations your anxious body and mind are experiencing. For example, if you are thinking, "I'm having a heart attack," you would remix that anxious track into something like this: "I'm not having a heart attack. My heart is beating fast because I'm scared. My heart is young and healthy and it can take a lot." Or you might jump to the conclusion that "I'm going crazy." You would remix that anxious track with a Jump Back like this: "I feel strange because I'm scared. People don't go crazy because they're having a panic attack!"

You will be able to float with panic if you can convince yourself (even a little) that these scary and uncomfortable feelings are not dangerous. In fact, we recommend that you use a Jump Back before you use other Floating tools. It is always easier to float when you have reminded yourself that the situation and your feelings are not dangerous. This kind of makes sense when you think about it. For instance, if you are afraid of dogs and a dog is sitting and looking at you, wouldn't it be easier to think about something else (distraction) and to calm yourself if you believed, even a little, that the dog was not going to bite you? The same is true for panic. It is always easier to hang out with scary or uncomfortable feelings if you believe, even a little, that they are not dangerous.

Calm Body Tools

Once you use a Jump Back, there are a handful of tools that you can use to keep yourself afloat. You can use the Calm Body tools. To recap, they go like this:

- Abdominal breathing—Breathe slowly and deeply, keeping it up for at least 5 minutes until you feel the Panic Wave going down.

- Visualization—Imagine a favorite calm memory or a peaceful place like floating on an inflatable raft in a warm pool or lying on the beach in Hawaii on a sunny day. If you like the raft image, imagine that you are on the raft as it goes gently up and down on the Panic Wave.

Distraction

Also, it can help to distract yourself from your anxious mind by doing something that requires you to concentrate. This can be hard to do at the first signs of feeling anxious or panicky, but once you have started, they can help. This can really help to keep your mind focused instead of panicking, and gives you a good chance to float. Remember, though, use your Jump Backs first, then distract yourself. Here are fun things teens do while they wait for the Panic Wave to go down:

- Read a magazine
- Do crossword or Soduko puzzles, or work on a jigsaw puzzle
- Knit, sew, or bead
- Play a card or board game with someone
- Play a musical instrument
- Listen to music or watch a favorite movie

Staying Afloat Talk

One of the most helpful strategies for keeping yourself afloat is to talk to yourself in a smart, supportive way to calm your anxious mind. In other words, you can remix your anxious tracks. We call this smart self-talk *Staying Afloat Talk*. We know that it helps teens to accept their feelings, to float on the Panic Wave, and to be patient while they wait for the wave to pass. Look at the Staying Afloat Talk below and use the ones that seem like they will help you the most. If you, your parents, or your psychotherapist has come up with other good ones, use those instead.

Once you get good at using a Jump Back and other strategies and tools, you will be able to combine them and float. But remember, always start with a Jump Back. For example, imagine breathing in while you are thinking, "I'm not having a heart attack," and breathing out while thinking, "My heart is beating faster because I'm scared." Then use our Staying Afloat Talk to calm your anxious mind while you ride the Panic Wave up and down. Or remind yourself that your heart is strong and healthy, and then distract yourself with something fun.

You have learned several tools, and all of them can work, but if you start with one tool that is difficult for you to use, switch to another one. If you get bored with one, pick another. Keep using your strategies and tools (Jump Backs, Calm Body tools, Distraction, or Staying Afloat Talk) until the Panic Wave subsides.

My Staying Afloat Talk

- I'm going to float with this anxiety and wait for it to go down.
- I can handle these feelings. They aren't dangerous.
- These feelings are uncomfortable, but I can manage them.
- I can feel anxious and still be in control of this situation.
- I'll just let my body do its thing. This will pass.
- It's okay to feel anxious. It's okay to float. It's okay to just be.
- I've floated on this wave before. I can do it again.
- I'm getting good at floating on my Panic Wave.
- This isn't dangerous. Nothing is wrong.
- This anxiety won't hurt me, even though it doesn't feel good.
- Nothing serious is going to happen to me. It never has before. I'm fine.
- This is just anxiety. I'm not going to let it get to me.

CREATING YOUR PANIC PLAN

Now it is time to put it all together and develop your own personal Panic Plan. One of the things teens tell us repeatedly is that while it is tough to face the Panic Wave, it is easier when they have a plan. Basically, a Panic Plan puts together all the pieces, all the things that you have learned and all the important things you want to remember when you begin to feel the Panic Wave building. If you want help, ask your parents or your psychotherapist to work with you to put it together. Once you have written your plan, put it somewhere you can find quickly when you feel the wave coming on.

1. First, think of your first signs of panic. If you are not certain, talk to your parents or your psychotherapist to get some ideas.
2. Consider your typical Mind Jumps to Panic and write out a list of your favorite Jump Backs.
3. Look through the Staying Afloat Talk and determine which might work for you. Record those in the plan.
4. Write down the Calm Body tools that you will use to combine with your Staying Afloat Talk and Jump Backs.
5. Lastly, find a place for your Panic Plan so that you know where it is when you want it. Remember, use your plan early and get ahead of the Panic Wave!

Take a look at the Panic Plan Darcy completed.

Darcy's Panic Plan

My first signs of the Panic Wave	The first sign of the Panic Wave is when I start to feel a little queasy. Then I start to worry I'm going to throw up (2 on the Anxiety Scale). When I really get nervous, I start to have trouble breathing and worry that I'm going to suffocate or die (4 on the Anxiety Scale).
My favorite Jump Backs	I'm not going to suffocate. I'm feeling short of breath because my neck and chest muscles are tight because I'm scared. I'm getting plenty of oxygen, it just feels like I'm not. My body knows how to breathe.
My favorite Staying Afloat Talk	I'm going to float with this anxiety and wait for it to go down. I've floated on this wave before. Nothing serious is going to happen to me. It never has before.
My favorite Calm Body tools	I can breathe to calm my mind and my body. I like to say "Fuzzy kitten" when I exhale.
Things I like to do to distract myself	Play my harmonica. Listen to my favorite song. Call Julie. She's my best friend.
Things people can do/say to help	My sister can play a board game with me if I ask. My mom can remind me that I can handle it. My dad can tell me that he's proud of me. That really helps because he gets anxious sometimes, too.

RIDING OUT PANIC

This chapter taught you how to detect when a panic attack is building and what to do about it. Keep in mind, you will be able to float with these scary and uncomfortable feelings if you can convince yourself (even a little) that they are not dangerous and then use tools to keep yourself a float. And, just like a real wave, the Panic Wave will go up and down. Be prepared for this, particularly when the wave is going down. Sometimes teens get anxious because the wave is going down and they expect that to continue. Then when, for no reason, the wave heads up again, this catches them off guard and they start panicking again. Try not to worry. Just keep floating on that wave as it goes up and down, up and down, and until it goes down for good.

My Panic Plan

My first signs of the Panic Wave	
My favorite Jump Backs	
My favorite Staying Afloat Talk	
My favorite Calm Body tools	
Things I like to do to distract myself	
Things people can do/say to help	

CHAPTER 7

FAMILY, FRIEND, AND SCHOOL STRESS

Do adults ever say to you, "Why are you so stressed out? This is the best time of your life," or "You're too young to be stressed." Teens, like adults, can feel stressed from time to time, no matter how great a life they have. Sometimes teens use "stress" to describe that they feel pressured or a bit under the microscope. Sometimes they use "stress" to mean that they are anxious or worried. Regardless, stress is really about feeling overwhelmed and finding it hard to cope. Like most teens, it can be hard for you to manage what your family, your friends, and your school expects and demands from you.

So, in this chapter, we list out common stressors for most teens, provide ideas about handling what stresses you, and describe some Stress-Busting tools. We also show you how to make a Stress-Busting Plan to help you deal with stressful situations as they pop up.

IDENTIFYING STRESS

Three types of stressors are common to all teens—family stress, friend stress, and school stress. These types of stressors occur often, sometimes on a daily basis, and can make your anxiety worse. And as you likely know, most family, friend, and school stress is unavoidable. It is just part of an active and full life.

The first step in learning to manage your stress is to know what stresses you. This way, you feel prepared when a stressor pops up, rather than surprised and overwhelmed. Also, being prepared will make it easier for you to use the four Stress-Busting tools we will talk about in this chapter. So, first, ask yourself: Is it stressful dealing with my family? Do I stress about my friends or social life? Am I stressed about getting good grades and or getting into college? If you answered "Yes" to any of these questions, it means you are experiencing some typical teen stressors. To help you figure out what stresses you, look at the list of 50 typical teen stressors. Review these stressors and notice if any of these exist in your life.

50 Typical Teen Stressors

Family

Visiting a parent who doesn't live with you	Caring for siblings
Curfew	Change in health of family member
Not spending enough time with family	Change in living situation
	Moving
Obligations at home (chores, family time)	Living in dual households
	Death of a parent
Fight with a parent	Parental divorce
	Visiting relatives

School

College applications	Bad class or teacher
Academic demands	Having teachers favor other students
Taking the SATs	
Homework or studying	Change in school
Bad grades	Start or finish of school year
Missing or being late to class	Getting ready for school

(continued)

50 Typical Teen Stressors *(continued)*

Friends

Dating
Peer pressure to drink or use drugs
Extracurricular demands
Fight with a boyfriend/girlfriend
Fight with a friend
Change in social activities
Meeting new people
Not spending enough time
with friends
Not having a boyfriend/girlfriend

Changes in friendships
Having few or no friends
Not getting along with a friend's
parents
Being in love or in a romantic
relationship
Loss of friendships
Sexual intercourse or other
sexual activities
Breaking up with a boyfriend/
girlfriend

Other

Pregnancy
Death of a relative or close friend
Changes in finances
Change in eating habits or dieting
Vacation
Getting punished at home or
school

Injury or illness
Getting fired from job or kicked
off athletic team
Outstanding personal
achievement
Change in sleeping habits

USING YOUR STRESS-BUSTING TOOLS

Knowing what stresses you can help you to feel alert, prepared, and possibly a little less stressed when these stressors occur. But to lower your stress further, you will want to learn some specific Stress-Busting tools. The four tools listed below have helped many teens and can help you manage routine stressors in your daily life, too.

These Stress-Busting tools include:

- Identifying your feelings
- Solving problems: ICAAN
- Asserting yourself: DEAL
- Negotiating a compromise

Identify Your Feelings

Identifying and noticing the telltale signs of stress can help to decrease stress before it gets out of hand. To see if you have any stress signs, ask yourself these questions:

- Are my muscles tight, and do they have me in knots?
- Do I feel jittery, jumpy, and fidgety?
- Do I have trouble falling or staying asleep?
- Have I lost my appetite, or am I craving junk food and overeating?
- Is my anxiety picking up?
- Have I noticed that I'm more irritable or short-tempered?
- Am I tired, fatigued, and feeling run-down?
- Am I having trouble concentrating?
- Am I quick to get tearful or feel extra emotional?
- Am I feeling like some things are out of control?

Do you have any of these stress signs? If you answered "Yes" to two or more of these questions, you are probably feeling stressed out. Once you have identified that you feel stressed, you can begin to do something about it. Believe it or not, sometimes just letting others know you are feeling stressed or anxious can decrease your stress levels. When others know how you are feeling, they sometimes can help, especially if they are the source of your stress.

Solve Problems: ICAAN

Many of the stressors listed earlier in "50 Typical Teen Stressors" are examples of problems you might have and want to solve. Situations such as being kicked off an athletic team for something that was not your fault, not having enough friends and feeling lonely, or feeling pressured by other teens to use alcohol or drugs can cause high levels of stress. These are definitely problems you would like to change. There are some easy-to-apply, step-by-step methods you can learn that may help you enhance your problem-solving skills. One very effective model has five steps that stand for ICAAN. These steps are:

> Identify your problem.
> Come up with a list of solutions.
> Assess the advantages and disadvantages to each solution.
> Apply your idea.
> Now, review how the solution worked and reward yourself for your effort.

To use ICAAN, do the following:

1. Identify and define the problem. A good way to do this is to ask yourself, "What's the problem? Why is it a problem? What is it that I'm trying to change?" If you are not sure exactly how to describe the problem, try asking others how they would define it.
2. Create a list of ideas that might solve the problem. Ask yourself, "How can I fix this?" It is best to brainstorm and come up with as many ideas as possible. (When brainstorming, quantity not quality matters!)

3. Assess and write out an Advantages and Disadvantages List for each idea. In other words, list the pluses and minuses for each idea. This will help you decide which idea(s) may be the best solution for your problem. (When looking at the advantages and disadvantages, go for quality not quantity.)
4. Apply your ideas and practice them. Choose a few solutions and try them out. Remember, you will not know if your solution works until you try it.
5. Now, review how your solution worked and praise yourself for your effort. If it did not work, then go back to your Advantages and Disadvantages List and pick another idea.

Assert Yourself: DEAL

Assertiveness is the third Stress-Busting tool you can use to lower your stress. Being assertive means letting others know how you feel and communicating what you want, while also considering the feelings and wishes of others. Unfortunately, assertiveness sometimes gets confused with *aggressiveness*. Being aggressive means you put your wishes ahead of the wishes of others, without regard for their feelings. The difference between the two is that being assertive includes the interests of many, whereas being aggressive includes the interests of one. Sometimes adolescents (and adults) try so hard not to appear aggressive that they skip over being assertive and go straight to being *passive*. Being passive means giving up your rights and not letting others hear your opinions, preferences, or ideas. Being passive can leave you feeling angry, resentful, and stressed. Neither aggressiveness nor passiveness will likely get you what you want. Sometimes even assertiveness will not get you what you want. But assertiveness gives you the best shot because the other two options leave you either being ignored or putting off other people.

As you know, many times the things that stress you most have to do with other people. When you are feeling stressed because parents or teachers are asking more and more from you, assertiveness can help you move a few things off your plate or, at least, to negotiate some time to complete those things on your ever-expanding to-do list. And when friends insist you do things that will only stress you out, assertively saying "No" helps you to take care of yourself. A tool that can help you become more assertive is called DEAL, which stands for Describe, Express, Ask, and List. DEAL can help you stand up for yourself, ask for help, and manage friendships, for example. It is important to use these steps in a calm and respectful way, without being aggressive or too pushy. To become more assertive, try using DEAL as follows:

1. Describe the problem. When you are talking to someone, tell her the problem. For example, "This is the third time you told me you would help me with my homework, but you keep bailing out at the last minute."
2. Express how the problem is making you feel. After you have described the problem, express how it makes you feel but without blaming the other person. For example, "Once or twice is okay, but bailing on me makes me think you don't care. It hurts my feelings, and it stresses me out because I have to find someone else to help me at the last minute."
3. Ask for a change. Once you have described the problem and how it makes you feel, ask for some change that you hope will fix the problem. Suggest a solution. For example, "How about if we agree that you don't say you're going to help me with my homework if you really can't?"
4. List how you think the change is going to improve the situation or fix the problem. This will motivate her to try out your idea. For example, "I think that if you tell me straight up that

you can't help me, I'll know that I need to get some help from someone else. And then I won't get upset with you anymore."

There are some situations where you might not feel comfortable being assertive, such as when dealing with an authority figure like a teacher, another adult, or an older teen. If this is the case, consider the disadvantages of not asserting yourself. If there are disadvantages, ask a friend or adult to assist you in asserting your position.

---

*My History teacher marked me down a grade for turning in a paper late.
When I explained I had finished it on time, she wouldn't listen.
I asked my English teacher for help, since he reviewed it for me but gave it back a day late. He and I talked to my History teacher. We resolved the situation, and I received full credit for the paper.*

—Ellie, age 14

Negotiate a Compromise

The final Stress-Busting tool is negotiation. *Negotiating* means helping two individuals or groups find a compromise when one of these individuals is you. *Compromise* helps to decrease conflict, and decreasing conflict will lessen your own stress as well as the stress of the other person. Take a moment to decide what you might be willing to give in a little on for a particular situation. Giving in, however, does not mean giving up. If you compromise a little, the other person will as well, and that way, you both win. Compromise does not work unless everyone in the discussion feels like they have gotten something and given something back.

To negotiate a compromise, follow these steps:

1. Make a T-chart on a blank piece of paper.
2. At the top of the left column, write "Things I could give a little on" and then write the things you could give a little on.
3. Next, at the top of the right column, write "Things I hold firm on" and list those things you want to stay firm on.
4. Then, look at what you listed as the "Things I could give a little on" and "Things I hold firm on" and see if you can find something between these ideas. This would be your compromise. Think carefully about both sides of the situation and then make a decision that satisfies everyone.
5. Finally, meet face to face and negotiate your compromise. Sometimes the first compromise does not work. Or you realize that you have given in more than the other person has, and it does not feel good. If so, go back to the chart, and review your ideas. Then, let the other person know that the first compromise did not work for you and that you would like to try again.

DEVELOPING A STRESS-BUSTING PLAN

Family, friend, and school stress affect the lives of all teens. Therefore, it is important that you learn to identify when you are feeling stressed and what tools you can use to lessen your stress, such as the four Stress-Busting tools described in this chapter. The Stress-Busting Plan below can help you identify what stresses you, as well as remind you to use any or all of the four tools to reduce your daily stress.

Take a look at the Stress-Busting Plan Clay created to deal with a fight he had with a his girlfriend.

Clay's Stress-Busting Plan

My stress: I had a bad fight with my girlfriend, Maria.

Identify my feelings	Irritable Increased anxiety Trouble sleeping Muscle tension and backache Trouble concentrating
Solving my problem **ICAAN** **I**dentify my problem **C**ome up with a list of solutions **A**ssess the advantages and disadvantages **A**pply my idea(s) **N**ow, review and reward	**I:** Maria and I fought because she says I don't spend enough time with her. **C:** 1) Eat lunch with Maria at school every day. 2) Study with Maria after baseball practice. 3) Make Saturday date night. 4) Call Maria before bed every night. **A: Advantages:** more time with Maria; Maria's happier; our relationship can develop. **Disadvantages:** less me time; less time with my friends; might feel suffocated; feel pressure to be with Maria all the time. **A:** Try some of the solutions listed above. **N:** Talking to Maria before bed every night and doing at least one thing together on the weekend worked really well.

(continued)

Clay's Stress-Busting Plan *(continued)*

Asserting myself DEAL	D: Maria, I think we spend enough time together, but you don't and it's upsetting you.
Describe my problem	
Express how it's making me feel	E: I'm upset we're fighting and I want to stay together. But I'm afraid of losing my independence and time with my activities and friends.
Ask for a change	
List how the change can help/fix my problem	A: How about we talk every night before we go to bed and do at least one thing on the weekend?
	L: That way, we'll talk a lot and will get to have a lot of time together each weekend.

Negotiating a compromise	Things I could give a little on:	Things I hold firm on:
	I can be more flexible with how I spend my weekends.	I want time to myself. I want to hang out with my friends.

TAKING ON YOUR STRESS

Let's face it—there will always be stress in your life. It can come from family, friends, and school. But knowing your stressors is your first step in dealing with it. And in this chapter, we provided you with some solid ideas on how to handle what stresses you by using some Stress-Busting tools. You can combine all of those tools to create your personal Stress-Busting Plan. Using your plan to take on whatever stressors life throws your way will allow you to calm your anxious mind and keep a handle on your emotions.

My Stress-Busting Plan

My stress: _____

Stress-Busting Tools

Identify my feelings	
Solving my problem **ICAAN** **I**dentify my problem **C**ome up with a list of solutions **A**dvantages and disadvantages **A**pply my idea(s) **N**ow, review and reward	
Asserting myself **DEAL** **D**escribe my problem **E**xpress how it's making me feel **A**sk for a change **L**ist how the change can help/fix my problem	

Negotiating a compromise	**Things I could give a little on:**	**Things I hold firm on:**

CHAPTER 8

NUTRITION, EXERCISE, AND SLEEP

Remember the Worry Wheel? It demonstrates how your anxious mind and your anxious body cause anxious actions. Anxious actions cause more anxiety, affecting your mind and body, and your Worry Wheel just keeps spinning. How can you keep your wheel from spinning out of control? In the previous chapters, we talked about how to calm your anxious mind to do just that. But what about your anxious body? How you take care of your body has a major effect on your mind and, consequently, on your anxiety. Are you eating right? Are you getting enough sleep? Are you exercising enough? All of these factors determine how you feel—and you can influence each of them. This chapter focuses on nutrition, exercise, and sleep and provides you with tools and information to improve on each so that you can calm your anxious body and mind.

EATING HEALTHY

Puberty is a period during which your body grows rapidly and requires more calories and nutrients. Teens need calcium to promote bone growth and protein to build muscle. And in high school, the academic and athletic demands of most teens increase, making it even more important that teens fuel their bodies with the proper nutrients. Unfortunately, you may have noticed that as the demands on your time, attention, and energy have increased, that it is more and more difficult for you to eat in a healthy way. You might skip meals, snack on sugary and processed foods, and eat on the go. When you fill your body with foods that are high in saturated fats, chemicals, and refined sugars or skip meals and eliminate key nutrients, your body cannot operate optimally and can leave you vulnerable to increased stress and anxiety.

Deciding what foods to include and what foods to avoid in your daily diet is a challenging task. Television, radio, magazines, and newspapers bombard most teens with dietary and nutritional advice, advertisements that promote convenience foods, and eating and dieting fads that come and go. At times, it can be difficult to know what or who to trust. In addition, you might feel pressured by friends to "fit in" and think about giving up a healthy lunch from home in favor of something from a vending machine, or dieting because you are worried about how you look. On top of that, a busy schedule that keeps you away from home for most of the day can make it difficult for you to eat healthy. So, the trick is to have a general plan of what you will eat each day and to try to eat healthy options whenever possible. Even small steps in this direction can improve your nutrition and, thereby, help you manage your anxious mind and body. This next section provides some basic recommendations from the American Academy of Pediatrics about how to improve your eating habits. (If you have significant concerns about your nutritional habits, a medical condition that requires dietary modifications, or if you believe you are over- or underweight, please talk to your physician or a nutritionist about your concerns.) Here we introduce several plans and strategies you might want to try.

Healthy Food Habits: DGA

Scientists and medical professionals have become increasingly concerned about the eating habits of North Americans, which they believe have contributed to a dramatic increase of obesity in both adults and youth. In response, the federal government has created Dietary Guidelines for Americans (DGA) to promote health and reduce risk for illness. The DGA outlines three important guiding principles. People are urged to:

1. Choose wisely from all food groups.
2. Strike a balance between what you eat and what you do.
3. Get the most nutrition from your calories.

The first principle encourages flexible and balanced meal planning with little if any restrictions. To achieve this, consider the rule of thirds as a quick and easy guide. One-third of your meal is protein (meat or beans), one-third is fruits and vegetables, and one-third is carbohydrates (grains and starch). In addition, include some oils and fats, and salt (which is often present in many foods), as well as foods with key vitamins and minerals, such as vitamins A and C, iron, and calcium. Current dietary guidelines recommend teens include up to 1300 mg of calcium daily. Most teens do not get as much calcium as their growing bodies need. Therefore, try to add some dairy into every meal and snack. If you are interested in additional guidance with meal planning, talk with your physician or a nutritionist.

The second principle encourages you to balance what you eat with what you do. Eat moderate sized portions and get a moderate amount of physical activity daily (see the section "Exercising to Calm Your Mind"). Eating large meals when you are not physically active is an example of your eating and activity level being out of balance. Similarly, restricting what you eat and exercising excessively is not balanced nor is it healthy.

The third principle emphasizes making smart choices that help you to get the most nutrition from what you eat. One Kit Kat wafer bar has 218 calories. Three part-skim mozzarella cheese sticks have 216 calories (72 each). However, cheese sticks will provide you with far more nutrition than a chocolate bar even though the calories may be the same.

A Balanced Diet: A Pyramid to Health

Another way to help you make healthy food choices would be to look at the U.S. Department of Agriculture (USDA) Food Pyramid and balance your diet accordingly. We bet you have seen this before. The pyramid recommends you include six food groups in your daily diet: (1) grains, (2) vegetables, (3) fruits, (4) milk, (5) meat and beans, and (6) oils and fats. Determining the amount of each food group to include in your daily diet varies according to your age, gender, weight, height, and activity level. To develop your own personalized plan, logon to the USDA's Web site and view the My Pyramid Plan located at www.MyPyramid.gov. Alternatively, if you want to get serious about eating healthier meals, speak to your parents about setting up an appointment with a nutritionist. Nutritionists are experts at helping teens create meal plans tailored to their particular needs.

Read a Food Label

Reading and understanding a Nutrition Facts food label can help you select the type and quantity of healthy foods to include in your meals and snacks. Food labels provide information about the nutrients in the food and the recommended percent daily value of each nutrient based on a 2000-calorie diet (although you may need more or fewer calories in your diet). Next time you pick up a package of food, check for the Nutrition Facts food label. It should be easy to find and is usually on the side or back of most food packages. The recommended serving size of the particular food is at the top of the label as well as the number of servings in each container. The label then lists the quantity of nutrients and vitamins found in a single serving of that food in grams or milligrams (1/1000 of a gram) and the percent daily nutritional value. Most foods contain fat, carbohydrates, protein, and fiber as well as vitamins A, C, and D, and minerals, such as calcium and iron. The purpose of the label is to provide you, the consumer, with a uniform method to plan the type and quantity of the foods to include in your meal or snack. In particular, check the food label for the amount of calcium in the food. Most teens get too little calcium, and the food label can help to make sure you get a sufficient amount of this important mineral in your diet each day. To learn more about how to read a Nutrition Facts label and to use these labels to plan your meals, speak with a nutritionist or your doctor.

Plan for Healthy Fast Food and Convenience Meals

Healthy fast food is possible! Foods you eat at home can sometimes be just as unhealthy and as high in saturated fats, salt, and chemicals as a fast-food double cheeseburger with all the fixings. While we are not recommending that you include fast food in your daily diet, it is reasonable to eat fast food on occasion, particularly if you make wise choices. For example, skip the creamy dressing on your salad and try oil and vinegar instead. Substitute a baked potato for fries, and drink milk or water instead of soda. Opt for a single burger without all the extra sauces or a baked fish filet. Finally, remember grandma's rule: everything in moderation. Grandma was right when she said it is best to eat a little of everything, rather than cutting certain foods out altogether. Depriving ourselves of certain foods can make us crave these foods and then eat too much of them when we give in. Making a lunch out of a burger, fries, and a shake, while not an ideal meal, is less harmful when eaten once a month versus once a day. Similarly, it does not help to eat too much only to starve ourselves for the rest of the day.

I knew I didn't want to cut out fast foods from my diet . . . I like chocolate shakes and fries too much to do that! But I also knew that too much of anything can be bad. So I decided to order a child-size shake and to split fries with a friend. Also, my friends and I are going to our school cafeteria salad bar for Friday lunch instead of grabbing fast food. My diet has improved and it's been easy. I don't feel like I'm missing out on my favorite foods.

—Ellie, age 14

Avoid Caffeine, Sugar, and Other Anxiety Irritants

You might be surprised to know that certain foods and substances can irritate your stress and anxiety. While not all teens are sensitive to these items, some teens discover that certain foods or substances can trigger physical reactions that feel much like the physical symptoms of anxiety, or make an anxious episode much worse. To ensure that your mind and body function well, we would like to review with you which foods can upset and irritate your body and can cause a range of unpleasant reactions, including anxiety or panic.

Caffeine is a stimulant that can trigger anxiety, irritability, or feeling revved up mere minutes after you ingest it. The physical symptoms that accompany that rush of too much caffeine can feel a lot like anxiety, and if you are anxious about feeling anxious, this can really get your Worry Wheel spinning. Interestingly, even low doses of caffeine from a chocolate bar or soda can cause you to feel shaky, increase your heart rate, and bring on a rush of anxiety if you are sensitive to this stimulant. In addition, certain food allergies can make you feel anxious, dizzy, irritable, confused, or moody. You may also get headaches and have trouble sleeping. These symptoms occur as the body attempts to fight off the offending substance and can happen several minutes to several hours after eating the item. Again, these symptoms are much like those that anxious teens experience during a panic attack or an intense anxious episode and can therefore trigger an escalation in your anxiety. If you suspect you have a food allergy or to learn more about which foods and substances might trigger symptoms like these, speak to your parents or your physician about how you might decrease or eliminate these foods or substances from your daily diet.

The final anxiety irritant is not really a food or a substance, but what can happen to your body when you have a lower than normal amount of glucose in your blood stream. This condition is *hypoglycemia,* also called low blood sugar. When your blood sugar level drops too low, you can feel a range of uncomfortable symptoms including feeling clammy or sweaty, dizzy, weak, and your heart can race. If you are thinking these symptoms sound like anxiety, you are right. These are some of the same symptoms people report in a panic attack or during an acute episode of anxiety. Hypoglycemia is common in people with diabetes but it can happen in people without diabetes. Typically, low blood sugar occurs several hours after a meal or first thing in the morning, when blood glucose levels are at their lowest. If you feel anxious and jittery a few hours after eating, in the middle of the night, or first thing in the morning, this could mean you are experiencing low blood sugar. When this happens, try eating something sugary and see if your symptoms go away. If you notice a clear pattern and find that eating something makes your symptoms decrease or go away altogether, we suggest that you speak to your physician who can determine whether you are hypoglycemic.

EXERCISING TO CALM YOUR MIND

If you are like most teenagers, you are not getting as much exercise as you used to when you were a kid. There are a couple of reasons for this. First, you are busier now than when you were 8 years old. You have more homework and a busier social life. Free time is harder to come by. Another reason teens exercise less is that by the time they get to high school, sports have become more competitive. Teens feel pressured to excel at a sport in order to play and dislike the stress of trying to make the team. Even though getting regular exercise is tougher now, exercise is still important. You know that a healthy body makes for a healthy mind, and vice versa. In fact, regular aerobic exercise actually changes your brain structure. Furthermore, along with looking and feeling better and stronger, exercise helps you to think more clearly and decreases stress and anxiety. Finally, aerobic activity can help your heart pump more efficiently, which can decrease *hypertension,* also known as high blood pressure. You might think high blood pressure only happens to adults, but you are wrong. More than five percent of kids and teens struggle with hypertension.

Like so many other things, just knowing something is good for you does not mean that you will do it. You might dread exercise and will avoid it at all costs. However, exercise does not have to mean that you run miles in gym class or swim 50 laps. A cardiovascular workout is 30 minutes of moderate exercise. Exercise can be fun and can include any physical activity you enjoy that gets your heart pumping. Review the list on the next page and pick three to five activities you might enjoy. Then decide when in your daily schedule you can commit to these activities. Be as realistic as possible—scheduling a one-hour hike in the woods after school when you already have a piano lesson, tutoring, and family dinner is unlikely to work. However, shooting hoops in your yard for 30 minutes might be a better fit with your schedule.

Archery	Horseback riding	Skiing
Aerobics	Household chores	Soccer
Badminton	Ice hockey	Softball
Baseball	Jumping rope	Squash
Basketball	Kayaking	Spin training
Bicycling	Lacrosse	Stair climbing
Body building	Martial arts	Strength training
Bowling	Mountain biking	Surfing
Canoeing	Pilates	Swimming
Cheerleading	Powerlifting	Table tennis
Crew	Racewalking	Team handball
Curling	Racquetball	Tennis
Dancing	Rock climbing	Track and field
Diving	Rodeo	Ultimate Frisbee
Fencing	Rollerblading	Volleyball
Field hockey	Rugby	Walking
Floor hockey	Running	Water aerobics
Football	Sailing	Water polo
Gardening	Scuba diving	Weight lifting
Golf	Shooting baskets	Windsurfing
Gymnastics	Shoveling snow	Wrestling
Handball	Skateboarding	Yard work
Hiking	Skating	Yoga

If you do not see an activity in the above list that sounds like fun, think of something you enjoy that meets the definition for a cardiovascular workout. For example, dodgeball and hula hooping are aerobic activities that qualify as exercise, as, does dancing in your room for 30 minutes. Get creative! Once you have chosen three to five activities, write them down at the end of the chapter using the My Health Plan.

GETTING YOUR Z'S

Does your alarm go off several times each weekday morning before you finally slide out of bed with your eyes glued shut? Do you feel as though you are in a fog for the first few hours of the school day? Do you often say to yourself, "I really should get more sleep. I just don't know how?" If you answered "Yes" to any of these questions, you are not alone. While experts say the average teen requires 9 or more hours of sleep per night to function optimally, the National Sleep Foundation's 2006 *Sleep in America* poll revealed that teens ages 11–17 are getting far less. Furthermore, the older the teen, the less sleep he or she gets. We know that one-half of high school seniors go to bed at 11 pm or later on school nights, and that most teens are awake for school at approximately 6:30 am. This amounts to an average of 7.5 hours of sleep per night. Although teens try to catch up with sleep on weekends, they average 8.9 hours sleep per night, which is still insufficient for the average teen.

Sleep expert, Dr. Mary Carskadon, describes the difficulty teens have in getting enough sleep as analogous to not filling up one's tank at night. Each day, teens start with a low or empty sleep tank with no opportunity to fill it back up during the day. Chronic lack of sleep can contribute to declining grades, lowered mood, increased anxiety, impaired athletic performance, and increased risk of motor vehicle accidents. We know your parents probably require you to go to bed early but also want you to do well in school and participate in an array of school (and after-school) activities that keep you up late each night. How can you do both? On top of that, television, online entertainment, and video games engage and activate your mind at a time when you should be shifting to a slower pace with less stimulation. Delayed sleep onset can contribute to a forward shift in the *circadian rhythm,* or internal clock, which leaves many teens feeling alert and active until well past 11 pm, making it difficult to get enough sleep before they must be up and ready for the day by 6:30 am. So, what are you supposed to do?

Know the Signs of a Low Sleep Tank

The first step toward improving your sleep is to be aware of the warning signs that your sleep tank is low. The National Sleep Foundation lists seven common signs that may mean you are not getting the sleep that your mind and body needs. Read this list and make a mental note of each one that applies to you.

- Difficulty awakening in the morning and yawning throughout the day.
- Trouble getting to school or being late to school on a regular basis.
- Relying on caffeine to remain alert and focused and to get through the day.
- Having trouble staying alert in school or falling asleep in class.
- Feeling more irritable, anxious, or angry on days when you have less sleep.
- Overscheduling yourself with too many academic and extra-curricular demands.
- Napping for more than 45 minutes each day or sleeping in on the weekends for more than 2 hours longer than a typical night.

If you experience several of these signs, it is likely that you are not getting enough sleep. Chronic fatigue is a real problem that requires attention. Other signs you should look for are snoring or having trouble breathing during sleep (symptoms of possible sleep apnea); experiencing leg cramps or tingling; or having prolonged insomnia that stops you from sleeping well. If you have any of these symptoms, talk with your physician. These might indicate that you have a sleep problem, which can also contribute to fatigue even if your sleep habits are good. You might even want to meet with a sleep specialist.

Keep a Sleep Diary

If you suspect you are not getting enough sleep or that you may have a sleep problem, the next step is to keep a sleep diary to learn more about your sleep habits. Once you know how much sleep you get each night and what factors might be interfering with obtaining an optimal 9 or more hours of sleep nightly, then you can begin to develop a more healthy sleep plan. What does your sleep schedule look like? It might be quite regular with the same bedtime every night. However, it could be erratic, staying up late to finish a school project one night, out late with friends another night, and then to bed very early the next night with the occasional nap squeezed in. Keeping a sleep diary for 1–2 weeks can tell you how much sleep you are getting, if it is enough sleep, and where you may be able to improve the quantity and quality of your sleep. Use the chart in the My Health Plan, at the end of this chapter to track your sleep and set some new sleep goals.

Learn Good Sleep Habits

The final step toward improving the quantity and quality of your sleep is to eliminate bad sleep habits. Some things may be obvious, such as eliminating caffeine or cutting back on certain activities if you try to pack too many academic, social, and extracurricular activities in each day. Here are a few tips from sleep experts that might help you create better sleep habits and a healthy sleep plan:

- Set a consistent bedtime and wake-time each day, including weekends.
- Do not drink any caffeinated beverages after lunch.
- Do not eat or snack 1–2 hours before bedtime.
- Exercise during the day but stop several hours before bedtime.
- Establish a relaxing bedtime routine beginning 1–2 hours before going to sleep. Turn off all electronic devices, as the ambient light from screens interferes in your brain's ability to slow down and prepare for sleep. Instead, read a book or magazine, listen to music, take a bath, or draw.
- Transform your room into an environment where going to sleep and staying asleep is easier. Install a lightproof shade or heavy curtains so that your room is dark, or wear an eye mask. Sleep comes as our bodies begin to cool, so make certain your room is nice and cool to help that along. Finally, use a fan to mask noises that might awaken you.
- Allow sleep to come naturally. If you cannot fall asleep within 30 minutes, do not fight it. Get out of bed and try a quiet activity such as reading a book or drawing. When you begin to feel drowsy, go back to bed. If you are still awake in 30 minutes, try this again.
- If you have a digital clock in your room, use a non-illuminating clock instead. It can be hard to fall asleep when you watch the clock, because you may worry about getting to sleep.
- Limit bedroom activities to sleep, engaging in all other "sleep stealers" such as watching television, doing homework, and talking on the phone to other areas of the home.

Do any of these strategies seem like something that you could try? You might want to ask a parent to help make some of these changes. Use the chart like the one at the end of the chapter in My Health Plan to write down the strategies that you want to include in your sleep plan.

I've made some changes to my nighttime routine that help me sleep better. I don't eat dinner later than 8 pm. I try to finish my homework by 10 pm. What I don't get to, I try to do in study hall the next day or make it up on the weekends when I have a little more time. I also turn off the computer and TV at least one hour before bed and opt for reading and listening to chill music to get me in the mood for sleep. Finally, I try to do all my homework in the family room so that my room is for sleeping, reading, listening to music, and hanging out with friends. This helps me think of my room as a calm, peaceful place to be rather than a place for stress and worry.

—Clay, age 17

DEALING WITH PRE-MENSTRUAL SYMPTOMS

Pre-menstrual symptoms (PMS) occur in up to half of all women and include both physical and psychological symptoms. Many of the psychological symptoms associated with PMS are the same ones that can occur during a panic attack or an acute episode of anxiety—anxiety, panic, tension, irritability, depression, moodiness, fatigue, and forgetfulness. To lessen the physical and psychological symptoms of PMS, make some small but significant changes in your daily schedule on the days leading up to and during your period.

Using a calendar, start monitoring your monthly cycle and notice whether your symptoms of panic (P), anxiety (A) and low mood (M) seem to get worse in the days leading up to your period. You can chart each symptom on a scale from 0–10 (0 = no symptoms – 10 = the worst symptoms ever) on a daily basis. For example: P = 3; A = 4; M = 6.

Make some changes in your eating habits, as well as exercise and sleep. These changes can help reduce your stress, anxiety and low mood during the days and weeks leading up to your period. Start by reducing foods high in sugar, salt, and fat, as well as cutting back on processed foods. Replace those foods with protein, whole grains, and fruits and vegetables. In addition, exercising can help increase metabolism and help your body effectively eliminate toxins that have built up during the month. This is especially important during the seven days prior to your menstrual cycle.

Do not cut back on your sleep. This is critical. Give your body extra rest when you can, and get a good night's sleep prior to and during your period. Although these suggestions may not eliminate all of the physical and psychological symptoms you experience, they can help reduce the impact these symptoms have on your daily life during the pre-menstrual phase. However, if your symptoms are more severe, or these suggestions do not provide much relief, talk to your physician or gynecologist about your situation.

DEVELOPING MY HEALTH PLAN

Now that you know more about the ways your body affects your mind and the value of eating well, exercising, and getting a good night's sleep, you are ready to design a personalized health plan. Use the following forms to generate nutrition and exercise goals, and goals to improve your sleep.

My Health Plan

Nutrition Goals

List below your old habits that you want to exchange for new habits	
OLD UNHEALTHY HABITS	NEW HEALTHY HABITS

Exercise Goals

List 3–5 activities you enjoy in the top box. Schedule your activities in the daily boxes below, aiming for about 30 minutes on most days.

My ideas are	
Monday	
Tuesday	
Wednesday	
Thursday	
Friday	
Saturday	
Sunday	

(continued)

My Health Plan *(continued)*

Sleep Diary

DAY	FELL ASLEEP AT	WOKE UP AT	TOTAL SLEEP TIME (in hours)	HOW I FELT TODAY (0 = exhausted – 10 = alert)
Monday				
Tuesday				
Wednesday				
Thursday				
Friday				
Saturday				
Sunday				

Average night's sleep: *Add up your hours for all 7 nights. Take this number, and divide it by 7. If you only tracked your sleep pattern for 5 nights, divide that number by 5, etc. You can track your sleep for a few weeks if your sleep schedule differs from week to week.*

My average night's sleep: ☐ hours.

Ideal average night's sleep: 8.5–10 hours.

My sleep goal is to get ☐ more hours of sleep per night.

Ideas to improve my sleep are:

1. _____

2. _____

3. _____

4. _____

5. _____

STAYING ON TRACK . . . MOST OF THE TIME!

Since anxiety is a mixture of what is going on in your mind and what is going on in your body, caring for your body is as important as caring for your mind. This chapter emphasized how good nutrition, moderate exercise, and sufficient rest can increase your physical and mental energy and reduce unwanted stress and anxiety. However, what happens if you cannot always stick to an optimal routine? Or what if you were in a groove but got off track because of a four-day weekend or a vacation?

First, do not beat yourself up if you slip a little. It is inevitable. Strive for flexibility not perfection. If you know in advance there will be a certain day or days when you cannot eat a balanced diet or cannot avoid foods high in saturated fats, refined sugars, and other chemicals (for example staying at Aunt Edna's for the weekend when her specialty is fried chicken and biscuits), then plan for it. Eat one piece of fried chicken instead of two. Grab a piece of fruit for a mid-afternoon snack instead of a biscuit and jam. Or if you have to skip your regular game of basketball because it is raining, consider an indoor exercise activity. However, if you just cannot think of a way to work through some problem, accept that for a few days your meal, exercise, and/or sleep plans will be less than ideal and then get back on track at the first opportunity. Sometimes the first opportunity is the start of a new day. However, it does not have to be. It can be in the middle of the day when you first notice you skipped breakfast or ate lunch from the vending machine, or when you realize you only had five hours of sleep the night before.

Be flexible and get back on track as soon as possible. If you assume the day is already a lost cause and wait until the following day, you have missed an opportunity to end the day on a good note. Furthermore, you might end up eating more unhealthy foods, lying around on the sofa for the rest of the day, or going to bed far too late simply because you did not plan the rest of the day. If you strive for a perfect health plan, you may find it difficult to maintain your plan for the long term, whereas if you are flexible and plan for occasional setbacks you will be better equipped to get back on track. This will help you to use My Health Plan well into the future.

CHAPTER **9**

STRAIGHT TALK
ABOUT MEDICATION

Sometimes, even though you have tried really hard to overcome your anxiety and worry on your own, you might decide you could use a little more help. Sometimes that means psychotherapy, and sometimes that means psychotherapy and medication. We have talked about when it would be beneficial to get extra help from a psychotherapist. So in this chapter, we will talk about medication. Specifically, we will describe how and when medication might help you and when it could become part of your plan to manage anxiety and panic. We will present several medication misconceptions you might have heard, things we feel that can get in the way of even considering medication. In addition, we will present information on the most common medications prescribed for anxious teens and help you to decide whether medication might be something you want to try.

WHEN MEDICATION MIGHT HELP

There are many reasons that you might want to try medication. Researchers have shown that the combination of medication and psychotherapy works better for many teens than either medication or psychotherapy alone. Medication helps you in the way a life jacket helps you. A life jacket helps you stay afloat. But the life jacket will not get you across the pool or back into shore. You do that. Similarly, medication can lower the intensity of your worry and fear a bit allowing you to use the tools in this book more successfully and slow your Worry Wheel.

What might make the most sense to you is this: If you have tried psychotherapy and you are still feeling very anxious or worried, you might try medication. If you are working really hard in your psychotherapy, but are having trouble getting some momentum going because everything you try feels like "one step forward and two steps back," you might try a medication. If you are having trouble getting to school and staying in class because you feel extremely anxious and panicky, you might consider medication to help you get through these tough periods. Or if you are depressed or have other things like attention-deficit hyperactivity disorder (AD/HD), you might want to try medication.

I've made great progress in facing my fear of germs, but my psychologist thought I could make a little more progress if I added some medication to my plan. When she first mentioned medication, I wondered if she thought I wasn't trying hard enough. But I was! And that's why I said no, at first. Plus I really wanted to do it all on my own and didn't want to cheat with medicine. My therapist talked to me about why taking medication isn't like cheating and the reasons why adding a medication to my plan might really help me be even more successful in managing my anxious mind. I decided that for me, there wasn't a whole lot to lose trying medication, so I started it. And you know what? After a month or two, I was feeling better. The combination of meds and therapy really worked for me.

—Min, age 16

COMMON MEDICATION MISCONCEPTIONS

Deciding to try a medication or not is a big deal, and later in this chapter, we will present strategies to help you and your parents make that decision. We will look at the pluses and minuses of taking a medication—and there are minuses, like side effects and health risks. But first, we want to give you the straight talk about medication. Sometimes teens will not try medication, because they believe things about medication that simply are not true. We call these medication misconceptions. Some kids might think:

- Using medication means I've failed.
- Using medication means I'm not in control.
- Using medication means I'm weak.
- Using medication will make me feel weird.
- Using medication will change my personality.
- Using medication won't help.

None of these is true! But go ahead and read about six common medication misconceptions, and let us help you sort out fact from fiction.

MEDICATION MEANS I'VE FAILED. Some teens may think that taking medication means that they have failed at psychotherapy or at managing the worry on their own. We do not see it that way. If you have been using this book or meeting with a psychotherapist, we know you have been working hard to overcome your anxiety and fearfulness. And learning to manage your anxiety and worry is not about winning or losing, or succeeding or failing. It is about deciding what will work best for your specific situation and then accepting the right kind of help so that you feel better.

Ask yourself whether you would think that your best friend was a failure if he tried medication. What would you say, "Yeah, you're a complete loser?" No, we do not think so. Instead, you would more likely be supportive, recognize the hard time he was having, and be really glad that he was willing to try something that just might help him feel better and get better. You might even admire his courage. So, if you decide to try medication, remember that it does not mean you have failed. It means that you are determined to get better and will consider all the options that your doctor and psychotherapist believe might help you accomplish your goals.

MEDICATION MEANS I'M NOT IN CONTROL. Sometimes teens will not try medication because they worry that the medication, in some way, will make them lose control. If you have heard this medication misconception, you might want to ask yourself, "Lose control of what?" If you are worried that you will not be in control of your body, you might discover that the medication makes you feel more in control of your body, not less. Many times, it is the anxiety itself that makes us feel that our body is out of control. If the medication decreases your anxiety, as your doctor hopes it will, then we think that you would likely feel in more control, not less. You can also consider the millions of people already on medication as evidence. Surely, if they were all not in control, we would hear about that!

MEDICATION MEANS I'M WEAK. Many times, teens will not try medication because they think it is a crutch or that it means they are cheating. These teens believe they should be able to handle their anxiety and worry on their own, and if they use medication, it means they are weak. Nothing could be further from the truth.

From time to time, we all use something to make the job of learning easier. Think about the first time you learned to ride a bike. You probably used training wheels to keep from falling so that you could learn to pedal, steer, and balance on the bike. When you first learned to swim, you might have used floaties to keep your head above the water. Did the training wheels help you pedal across the parking lot? Did the floaties get you across the pool? Of course not! You did those things. Not the training wheels. Not the floaties. You probably can think of many other examples of how people use certain things to help them learn a skill or make things a little easier. Medication is a little like training wheels or floaties. It helps make things a little easier while you learn how to manage your anxiety and worry, using the Calm Mind and Calm Body tools in this book or the tools you may learn in psychotherapy.

MEDICATION WILL MAKE ME FEEL WEIRD. Sometimes teens worry that medication might change them in some important way or that they will feel weird or different. This is true. Medication, if it works, will make you feel different and maybe even act different. But this is because you will feel less anxious and act less fearful. Being less anxious can feel unusual to you. After all, if you have been anxious for many years and then you begin to feel calm, it can be a strange experience. Although some of the side effects might feel different, most of these go away within the first few weeks of being on the medication.

MEDICATION WILL CHANGE MY PERSONALITY. This might be hard to talk about, but some teens worry that medication will change their personality. They worry that medication might make them less fun, less creative, or dumb them down. This is a big medication misconception. Think about the times when you are not anxious. That is the relaxed, talented, and confident you. The relaxed, talented, and confident you are parts of your personality, too. Anxiety keeps those parts of you hidden more than you might like. Medication will not change your personality. Instead, medication may get the anxiety out of the way so that the hidden parts of you can shine through.

MEDICATION WON'T HELP. The last common misconception teens have is that medication will not help. This is a misconception because we know that medication helps most teens. For some teens medication helps a lot, and for some teens medication helps less. The real question—and it is a fine one for you to ask—is, "Will medication help me?" Your doctor, your parents, and even you will not know the answer to this question unless you give medication a good and fair try. The misconception that medication will not help can really get in the way of you answering this question. Sometimes you believe this misconception because you are depressed and believe that many things will not work out for you. If this is the reason, medication could really turn things around for you. Again, there is no way to know unless you try it. Your doctor, psychotherapist, or parents can help you feel more hopeful about the chances of medication helping you. Talk to them and see what they say.

Do you have any of these medication misconceptions? Look at the following list and circle "Yes," "No," or "Maybe" for any of the medication misconceptions that are getting in your way. If you have a medication misconception that is not on the list, write it down and take it to your parents or your psychotherapist so that you can examine this misconception and get all the help you deserve.

My Medication Misconceptions

Directions: Circle Yes, No, or Maybe for all your medication misconceptions.

Medication means I've failed.	Yes	No	Maybe
Medication means I'm not in control.	Yes	No	Maybe
Medication means I'm weak.	Yes	No	Maybe
Medication will make me feel weird.	Yes	No	Maybe
Medication will change my personality.	Yes	No	Maybe
Medication won't help.	Yes	No	Maybe
Other:	Yes	No	Maybe
Other:	Yes	No	Maybe

MEDICATIONS USED FOR ANXIETY

It can be overwhelming to read a long list of different medications. The bottom line is this: If you decide to try a medication, there are many choices, allowing you and your doctor to find one that will work well for you. If you are interested in learning more about medications, check out the Additional Resources section at the end of the book for a list of books and Web sites that provide more detailed information. In particular, the U.S. Food and Drug Administration (FDA) provides the most current information about these and other medications.

SSRIs

The most common type of medication used for anxious teens is a type called *selective serotonin reuptake inhibitors (SSRIs).* Doctors often prescribe SSRIs for anxious or depressed individuals. Interestingly, anxiety and depression involve many of the same changes in brain chemicals, so medications that target these brain chemicals often work for anxious or depressed minds. Researchers think SSRIs boost the activity of *serotonin* (a brain chemical or neurotransmitter) in your brain. SSRIs include citalopram (Celexa), escitalopram (Lexapro), fluoxetine (Prozac), fluvoxamine (Luvox), paroxetine (Paxil), and sertraline (Zoloft). Usually, your doctor starts you at a low dose of an SSRI and slowly increases the dose over several weeks. For this reason, it can take a few weeks for you to feel the full effect of these medications. During these first few weeks, you might experience side effects, which tend to be mild for most teens.

Different SSRIs can have different side effects. For example, some teens feel sped up or overly energized on sertraline and fluoxetine but feel calmer and even sedated on fluvoxamine and paroxetine. At times, when your doctor starts you on an SSRI or increases the dose, you might start to feel physically restless or revved up. Other possible side effects include nausea, headache, nervousness, trouble sleeping, jitteriness, and rashes. Sometimes teens will experience sexual side effects on these medications but are too embarrassed to talk about this with their doctor. Whatever the side effect, we hope you will talk with your doctor about it and any other changes in the way you feel. Again, not all teens respond to the SSRIs in the same way nor do they all experience the same side effects. Doctors are very good at helping teens either manage these side effects or find another SSRI with less intense side effects that works for them.

SNRIs

Another and newer type of antidepressant medication used to treat anxiety is the *serotonin-norepinephrine reuptake inhibitor (SNRIs)*.

These medications, like the SSRIs, work on serotonin but also work on another brain chemical called *norepinephrine*. SNRIs include venlafaxine (Effexor) and duloxetine (Cymbalta). The side effects of these medications are similar to those of the SSRIs, and like the SSRIs, these medications can take several weeks before you get the full benefit of the medication. Scientists have not studied these medications as much as the SSRIs for treating anxiety in teens. However, they appear to be as safe as the SSRIs, and teens tend to handle the side effects pretty well.

Benzodiazepines

Benzodiazepines are another kind of medication that specifically targets anxiety. These medications work more quickly than the SSRIs, and if you try them, you might notice that you feel less anxious almost immediately. Benzodiazepines work well to cut a panic attack short, but they are not nearly as good as antidepressants at stopping the next panic attack from occurring. Therefore, doctors often prescribe a benzodiazepine together with an antidepressant early on, while waiting for the antidepressant to reduce anxiety overall. Researchers think benzodiazepines work by increasing the levels of *gamma-amino-butyric acid (GABA)*, another neurotransmitter, in your brain. Benzodiazepines include alprazolam (Xanax), chlordiazepoxide (Librium), clonazepam (Klonopin), diazepam (Valium), and lorazepam (Ativan).

Some teens tell us that benzodiazepines make them feel drowsy or make it hard for them to pay attention in school. Other side effects include fatigue, confusion, or loss of coordination. In addition, your doctor may tell you that you cannot take this medication and drive, too. Usually, the doctor will prescribe a benzodiazepine to help you get you through a difficult period of anxiety or panic, but generally will not recommend you take these medications for more than a few months. That is because some teens (although not many given the number of teens who are actually prescribed benzodiazepines) become dependent on these medications and need higher and higher doses to get the same effect. For these and other reasons, benzodiazepines are not usually the first thing doctors think to try with teens, unless they are having frequent and intense panic attacks. If your doctor does recommend benzodiazepines, you will want to make certain you and your doctor work closely together to monitor how they affect you.

Buspirone

Depending on how you respond to these medications, your doctor might suggest another medication called *buspirone (Buspar)*. This medication works more like a benzodiazepine than an SSRI, and it seems to relieve anxiety and depression in adults. Although we do not have a lot of information about how well they work with teens, many doctors think this medication can help teens and might be worth a try because most teens experience few side effects on it. It can take several weeks for this medication to begin to work. It is not particularly helpful if your anxiety is high and it is often not enough by itself. If that is the case, your doctor might decide that an SSRI is a better choice for you. In addition, doctors will often add buspirone to an SSRI because it can sometimes boost the effect of the SSRI. This can mean that you experience the same benefit on a lower dose of SSRI, which can mean fewer and less intense side effects.

TCAs

Sometimes doctors will recommend an older type of antidepressant medication called *tricyclic antidepressants (TCAs)* to treat anxiety disorders. These medications, like the SNRIs, work on the concentration and activity of serotonin and norepinephrine in your brain. But teens usually experience more troublesome side effects on these medications than on the newer medications. For that reason, the TCAs are not the first medication your doctor is likely to consider to help decrease your anxiety. TCAs typically prescribed for teens include amitriptyline (Elavil), clomipramine (Anafranil), desipramine (Norpramin), imipramine (Tofranil), and nortriptyline (Pamelor). Because these medications can sometimes affect the electrical system in your heart or increase the risk of seizures in some teens, your doctor will want to monitor the concentration of these medications in your blood to make certain you are on an appropriate dose. In addition, your doctor might want you to have an EKG or ECG (electrocardiogram—a simple test to see that your heart is operating okay) before they prescribe a TCA, and repeat this procedure periodically for as long as you are taking the medication. Although most teens do not experience these more serious problems, you likely may have such unpleasant side effects as dry mouth, constipation, dizziness, drowsiness, and blurred vision.

WHAT YOU CAN EXPECT

It is tough to tell you what to expect exactly when you start a medication because different teens respond differently to the same medication. Things like your age, sex, weight, and body chemistry can make a big difference. However, the most important thing to remember is that it can take time before you begin to feel better. For the SSRIs, it can take 4 to 6 weeks for you to feel the full effect of the medication if it is working. So, it is important to be patient and give the medication a full try. Also, your doctor will want to start slow and work the dose up so that you do not have too many side effects. Furthermore, do not assume the first medication you try will be the one for you. Sometimes that is true, but it is possible that you will have to try another before you find just the right one. Plus, it takes time to get the right dose. If an SSRI works for you, your doctor will likely want you to stay on it for 9 to 12 months, maybe even longer. That gives you time to work hard to learn to handle your anxiety with the help of the tools in this book and your psychotherapist.

Shortly after I started taking my medication, I noticed I felt more jittery and nervous than I usually do. I also had a mild headache that never seemed to go away. It was weird, and at first I decided to deal with these things on my own. But then I mentioned this to my mom, and we talked to my doctor. Turns out, the jitters and my headaches were normal side effects caused by the type of medication that I was on and that they would stop after a few weeks. I'm glad we spoke to her, because knowing that they were normal side effects made everything easier to handle.

—Min, age 16

All medications can cause unwanted effects in addition to the desired ones. For example, even something as mild as aspirin can give some teens a rash. Some teens do not feel any side effects on antidepressant or antianxiety medications at all. It really depends on the teen. If you start a medication, let your doctor know during your check-ups how you are feeling and answer your doctor's questions as honestly as you can. Remember, you are the expert on you, and your doctor cannot help you if he does not know how you are feeling.

All antidepressant medication (whether SSRIs, SNRIs, or TCAs) can cause mania in teens who are vulnerable and at risk for bipolar disorder. *Mania* is a state that is somewhat like the opposite of depression—happy or irritable mood with increased energy, decreased need for sleep, and feeling as though you are invincible. These can seem like great traits. But in excess, they produce real problems. A family history of bipolar disorder increases the likelihood of mania, but medication-induced mania can occur even without a family history.

You may have read some scary stories about the increased risk of suicide by some teens taking paroxetine (Paxil) for anxiety. The FDA investigated this and found that it was really not clear whether antidepressant medications significantly increases suicidal thoughts in teens. The FDA has since recommended that antidepressant medications have a label that warns about the possible danger of increased suicidal thoughts and urges. Be sure to talk with your doctor about this issue and if there are risks for you.

DECIDING TO TRY MEDICATION OR NOT

Deciding whether to try medication is a tough decision for many teens. To help yourself through this process, think about and jot down the pluses and minuses of taking medication. It won't take too long to do and may really help you with decision. If your parents have already talked to you about medication, then you could do this with them. They probably have already spoken to a doctor or even other parents of teens who are taking medication. They might have some good ideas about pluses or minuses that have not occurred to you. Take a look at Min's Pluses-Minuses List, and then try it on your own.

Min's Pluses-Minuses List

Pluses to taking medication	Minuses to taking medication
• My mom told me Stephanie tried a medication for her anxiety and it really helped, so maybe it would help me too. • I'm working really hard in my therapy but sometimes facing a fear is just too scary for me. Maybe, like my therapist said, a little medication might make therapy a bit easier for me, and I can be even more successful. • Sometimes, I feel like the anxiety is wearing me down. Maybe a medication would help me feel less worn down.	• If my friends found out I was taking a medication, they might think I was some sort of mental case. • If I tried medication, then I'd have to admit that I really have a problem with anxiety. • I might have some side effects. • It's a hassle to take medication and one more thing my parents have to remind me to do. Plus it might not work.

To make your own Pluses-Minuses List, follow these steps:

1. Use a T-chart to draw two columns in the middle of the page.
2. At the top of the left-hand column, write "Pluses to taking medication." In that column, list all the benefits you can think of to taking a medication. At the top of the right-hand column, write "Minuses to taking medication." In that column, list all the drawbacks or downsides you can think of to taking a medication.
3. Finally, read both lists and see if a decision stands out. At the bottom of your list, write your decision. If you are still unsure, consider reviewing your list with your parents, psychotherapist, or your support person.

Talking to Your Parents About Medication

If you think you might want to give medication a try, the first step—if you have not done it already—is to talk to your parents about it. Because anxiety is something that is inside you, your parents may not know just how anxious you are. Let them know. Sometimes teens are more ready to try medication than their parents are. That is okay. If you are worried about bringing up the topic, talk it over with your psychotherapist, if you have one, or your support person, like a school counselor or your doctor. If talking to your parents still makes you nervous, ask whether your support person might be willing to meet with you and your parents to discuss the pluses and minuses of medication for you. This person might be able to help you and your parents talk it through and come up with the decision that is best for you. You can use your Pluses-Minuses List to get the conversation going.

Working With Your Parents and Doctor

If you decide to try medication, the next step is to put together a team. Of course, there is you and your parents, but another major team member is the doctor who will prescribe the medication. Prescriptions can be written by your family doctor and sometimes other medical professionals. Sometimes your family doctor will not feel comfortable writing a prescription for an antianxiety or antidepressant medication and will refer you to a psychiatrist. This happens quite often and it does not mean there is something seriously wrong with you. Psychiatrists are medical doctors just like your physician, except that they specialize in the diagnosis and treatment of mental health disorders. They have the most knowledge and training in antidepressant and antianxiety medication and many have special training in working with teens.

Usually, you will meet with the doctor first for an evaluation, and if the doctor (and you and your parents) thinks medication might help, the doctor will discuss with you and your parents any potential risks and side effects of the medication and start you on one. In addition, the doctor will want to know if you have allergies (some allergy medications interact with antianxiety or antidepressant medications) and whether you are taking any other medications (prescription, over-the-counter, or herbal supplements) because sometimes one medication interferes with another. Finally, your doctor may want to know about your drug and alcohol use. It is important that you are honest about this topic because some medications interact dangerously with alcohol and drugs. If you are scared that your doctor will tell your parents, ask the doctor to tell you what she will and will not share with your parents. This can help you feel more comfortable. In addition, it is perfectly okay for you to ask to meet with your doctor alone, if you want. Many teens do, and many doctors encourage this.

If the doctor prescribes an antidepressant, the doctor will likely start you on a low dose and ask to meet with you again in a few weeks to check in and hear how you are doing. Because you know your body better than anyone does, your doctor will want to know how you are feeling during your check-up appointments. Let your doctor or parents know right away if you start to feel better or worse. Remember, most mild side effects often go away in a few days, so hang in there.

A FINAL WORD

Deciding to take medication can be a tough decision—a decision that you will want to come to on your own and to base on facts and information. After reading this chapter, you might be ready to try medication. Or you might want to think about it some more. That is fine. It is important not to feel rushed into such a big decision. If you're on the fence about whether to take medication or not, try reading over the chapter a few more times, or discussing your concerns with your parents, psychotherapist, and perhaps even some trusted friends. This can really help.

CHAPTER **10**

HOPE, HEART, AND HEADS-UP

By now, you have learned some tools to help you calm your anxious mind and your anxious body. Perhaps you have had days or weeks in which your anxious mind is less anxious and your anxious body is calm. Congratulations! It is not easy. It takes time and practice. In this final chapter, we invite you to look back on what you have learned and accomplished so that you can plan your next step. We hope you are feeling less anxious and fearful and that you will remain that way.

But as you know, life is stressful from time to time. And when life is stressful, your anxiety may try to make a comeback. This is normal. The tools you have learned will help you manage your anxiety. However, we believe that as important as the Calm Body and Calm Mind tools are, it is important for you to have a positive, proactive attitude that will help you manage your anxiety over the weeks and months to come. This attitude is made of hope, heart, and heads-up. After we talk about those, we describe how to build your own Wellness Plan, which includes the tools you have learned as well as your new attitude toward your anxiety and fear, to keep your anxious mind from making a comeback.

LIVING WITH HOPE

Hope is having confidence that things will work out okay, and nothing builds confidence more than success. Take a few minutes now and review what you have learned and what tools have been the most helpful. What goals did you set for yourself and which ones did you accomplish? Perhaps over the last few weeks and months you have used some of the tools to overcome a fear or calm your anxiety a bit. Perhaps the tools have helped decrease the frequency of your panic attacks because you worry less about having one. Perhaps you are managing your school or friend stress a little better and are feeling more hopeful that things will work out okay there, too.

Yes, as the saying goes, nothing succeeds like success. If you are unsure about what you have accomplished, ask a parent or friend if they have noticed any changes. (You do not need to tell them that you were using the book to get some feedback.) Ask them, "Do I seem a little less anxious or worried to you? Have you seen me try-ing things that I used to avoid? Do I seem a little more confident?" Reward yourself for what you have accomplished. The reward can be a simple a pat on the back, "You know what? I worked hard and it wasn't easy, and I'm pleased with what I accomplished." Alternatively, you might schedule a fun activity with your family or a friend to celebrate.

However, in spite of your hard work, you may continue to feel very anxious some of the time or even most of the time. Sometimes teens might use all the tools in the book, practice hard, and still have trouble managing their anxiety. If this is the case for you, it may be time to get some extra help. You could ask a parent to work with you on the tools in this book or meet with a psychotherapist to learn a few more tools. You could talk to your pastor, rabbi, doctor, or other helping professionals. (If you are thinking of asking for some extra help, we suggest you re-read Chapter 2 that discusses *Who and How to Ask for Help.*)

HAVING HEART

Heart means living your life as fully as you can. As you know, anxiety can rob you of heart, as well as fun, and can really take up a lot of space in your life. Perhaps you have felt too anxious to try new things that sound like fun. Perhaps you have wanted more friends but have felt too worried to do the things that would help you meet new teens and develop new friendships. Perhaps you would like to have a girlfriend or boyfriend but your anxiety has made that seem impossible, too. If you are having trouble imagining a life with less anxiety and worry, try to visualize it. Use the visualization tool from Chapter 3 to see a life you would like to have. Imagine how it would feel to be less anxious or frightened. Would you sleep better or be less concerned about your diet and appearance? Imagine all the activities you might try or the areas of your life in which you might act differently—school, sports, friendships, family, and more. What would change or be different for you if your anxious mind played less of a role in your life? Would you like to

- Join an athletic or recreational club?
- Make new friends?
- Go on a date?
- Learn to drive?
- Apply for a summer internship?
- Travel abroad?

Just taking a few moments to visualize what you want can actually increase the likelihood that you will get it.

---

*I see myself sitting in class and raising my hand to share things that I know.
I won't worry much about what my teacher or the other kids think. I'll smile
at kids when I see them and spend more time hanging out. I'll have a girlfriend and lots of good friends. I won't be the most popular kid in the
school, but I'll have my close friends and I'll feel fine!*

—Bobbie, age 15

GIVING YOURSELF A HEADS-UP

As we have mentioned, calming your anxious mind is not easy, but we
believe that the tools in this book can help. However, no matter how
successful you have been, anxiety might be looking to make a comeback. This means that it is essential that you stay alert. You can give
yourself a heads-up by being prepared for a comeback. That is where
your Wellness Plan comes in. Your Wellness Plan is the way you can
calm your anxious mind over the long haul so that you can hold onto
the gains you have made. Your Wellness Plan includes five things:

- Knowing the difference between lapse and relapse.
- Knowing what stresses you and how to plan for them.
- Knowing the tools that calm your anxious mind and body the
  most.
- Knowing how to check in.
- Knowing who to ask for support and calling on them.

KNOW THE DIFFERENCE BETWEEN LAPSE AND RELAPSE. Whether
you have calmed your anxious mind a little or a lot in using this
book, you will still have days when your mind will jump to an
anxious track, and you will talk yourself into feeling nervous
or afraid again. Many times, the anxiety you feel is normal. For

example, most teens will feel slightly anxious in anticipation of a state championship game, driving during a snowstorm, or taking a college entrance exam. This type of anxiety is helpful. It can improve your performance, as in the case of driving in the snow or playing in a big game, and tends to decrease once it has done its job of preparing and protecting you. However, sometimes anxiety lasts for more than the length of a specific stressor, continuing for days, weeks, or even months. If this happens, it might mean that your anxiety is trying to launch a comeback. There are two ways your anxious mind launches a comeback: through a lapse or through a relapse.

A *lapse* is a minor setback that lasts for no more than a few days or a week. Typically, lapses have little impact on your life. You might notice it is slightly harder to focus on schoolwork; you are a little more irritable, jumpy, or tense; and perhaps it takes longer to fall asleep. But you are still able to attend school, socialize with your friends, and continue to do most of your activities. A lapse might begin when your Worry Wheel starts spinning in response to a minor stressor, but then lingers after the stressor stops, spinning from one worry to another so that you find yourself having the worry of the day. Most teens (and adults, too) are vulnerable to a lapse if they have stopped using their Calm Mind and Calm Body tools on a regular basis. However, the good news is that if you use your tools right away, you can quickly turn a lapse around, calm your anxious mind, and slow down your Worry Wheel. Most teens manage lapses well without additional help from others. However, sometimes a lapse can last for more than just a few days, extending into weeks and even months. This might be a sign that your lapse has now morphed into a relapse.

A *relapse* is a major setback, because it lasts for more than a week, and typically has a moderate to severe impact on your life. If this happens, you might notice that because you are feeling more anxious, you are starting to miss school or that you are having trouble completing your homework. Many nights it may be difficult for you to fall asleep because your Worry Wheel is spinning, or you wake during the night and have trouble getting back to sleep. You may have stopped hanging out with friends or attending family outings because you feel anxious. You may notice that it is getting more and more difficult to do the things that a few weeks ago you did with ease. Unlike a lapse, a relapse may require help from others such as a psychotherapist or counselor. At times, your anxious mind will launch a relapse when you experience a major life stressor such as your parents divorcing, a death in the family, when you leave for college, or if you or a loved one has a major medical illness.

KNOW WHAT STRESSES YOU. You might have noticed that stress stirs up your anxiety. This is true for everybody, and since we cannot prevent stress, the best we can do is prepare for it. Knowing which stressful situations tend to stir up your anxiety can help you prepare for them. Everyone operates this way. When you start a new school year, a new job, or a new friendship, you prepare for it. For example, in the weeks leading up to a new school year, you might go shopping for school supplies and new clothes, or you might inform your boss that you can no longer work weekday mornings. Preparing for stressful events (even exciting ones) is one way we can keep the Worry Wheel from spinning into high gear.

The first step in preparing for a stressful event is to know what events typically get your Worry Wheel spinning. Think about the situations in which you used to feel anxious (or still get the Worry Wheel spinning a little), as well as other situations that your friends tell you stress them out. If you used to (and perhaps still do) get really anxious in crowded places, you might list school assemblies as a situation where your anxious mind might launch a comeback. In addition, consider any changes or big transitions that might happen in the next weeks or months, such as starting a new school year, switching schools, or going away to college, since these situations typically stir up the anxious minds of most teens. Final exams, tests like the SAT, or competitions like the basketball playoffs can stir things up, too. Take some time now and think about any stressful situations you might experience in the next twelve months. Go ahead and add them into the "Situations that might launch a lapse or relapse" box in the My Wellness Plan at the end of this chapter.

KNOW THE TOOLS THAT HELP. Knowing which situations tend to increase your anxiety will help you prepare for it. Think about the things you have learned that have helped you calm your anxious mind the most. You might have felt relieved to learn in Chapter 1 that feeling anxious is not a sign of weakness, but a protective response that has gone awry. You might want to remember that it is better to float with a panic attack than it is to fight it or that you were able to face your fears once and that you can do it again. We suggest you write these things down now in the "Important things to remember" box in the My Wellness Plan. Do this when your anxious mind is calm, and you are thinking smart, so that you are more likely to believe the wise things you have written when something stirs up your anxious mind.

Next, list the tools that are the most helpful in calming your anxious mind. If you have felt calm for many weeks or months, you may not have even thought about these tools or which tools helped to calm your anxious mind the most. Also, take a look at the Worry Wheel. Here we have included the tools that can help calm your anxious mind, body, and actions.

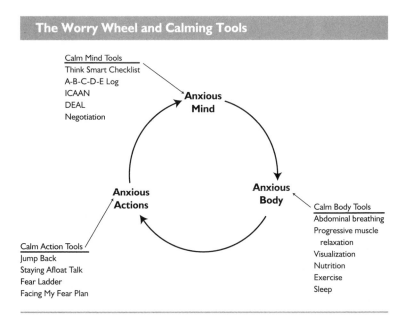

The Worry Wheel and Calming Tools

Calm Mind Tools
Think Smart Checklist
A-B-C-D-E Log
ICAAN
DEAL
Negotiation

Anxious Mind

Anxious Actions

Anxious Body

Calm Body Tools
Abdominal breathing
Progressive muscle
  relaxation
Visualization
Nutrition
Exercise
Sleep

Calm Action Tools
Jump Back
Staying Afloat Talk
Fear Ladder
Facing My Fear Plan

Listing these tools in your Wellness Plan now can help you quickly know what to do to calm your anxious mind if you need to. Go to the My Wellness Plan at the end of this chapter and look at the box labeled "My Favorite Tools." Circle all the tools in this book that helped you calm your anxious mind. It is okay if you did not like all of the tools or if some of them were not particularly helpful. Circle only those tools that are your favorites. If you do not remember a particular tool or how it works to calm your anxious mind, just take a mini-refresher course and re-read the description of the tool.

KNOW HOW TO CHECK IN. Just like most of the things you have learned to do, practicing at least periodically is the way you stay good at it. Managing your anxious mind is no different. If your anxious mind is calmer, and you have started to face your fears one step at a time, we want to provide you with some tips on how you can continue this process and keep your anxiety small and manageable. Although the tips we recommend involve some work and effort on your part, it pays off to practice a little every day or week. Think of this as a way to check in with yourself. Review the following list and make a mental note of those ideas you believe are realistic for you to try in the upcoming weeks and months:

- Set aside 10–20 minutes once a week for the next six months and once a month for the next six months to do the following:
  - Review your Wellness Plan.
  - Predict potential stressors you may face in the upcoming week and pick one or more Stress-Busting tools to use if needed.
  - Plan your nutrition, exercise, and sleep goals for the upcoming week.
  - If panic is still a part of your anxious mind, review your Panic Plan. If you are no longer experiencing panic attacks, consider reviewing your plan periodically, such as once or twice a month, to remind yourself of the main ideas.
- Practice your deep breathing, muscle relaxation, or visualization tools prior to or during routine stressors you encounter each week. Common stressors include taking a test, being late, dealing with a lot of homework, arguing with a friend or family member, and getting a bad grade.
- Notice anxious tracks playing in your anxious mind at least once a week, and use the A-B-C-D-E Log to remix them. If you no longer hear anxious tracks, listen for examples that others might have. Then, remix those just to be certain you can still do it!
- Pay attention to urges or plans to avoid your fears and face them! Consider carrying a stack of index cards in your backpack

or purse or keeping a journal. Each time you catch an urge or plan to avoid, write out, "The thing I want to avoid is . . . ," and then, "But what I will do instead is. . . ."

Did you choose a few of these ideas? Are you committed to trying them? The more ideas you choose and the more committed you are to trying them, the greater the chance your anxiety will stay small and manageable. Although it might seem like a lot of work, you will find that as you start to make a regular habit of doing check-ins and using your favorite tools, the more it will feel like a routine part of your life, no different from brushing your teeth or doing homework.

Furthermore, be flexible. If you go on vacation, you also might want to have a vacation from using your tools. This might be a good decision if vacations do not tend to stir up your anxious mind. Or if you have a busy week and forget to do your check-in, reschedule it for another day. Or if you forget to do a track remix for a few weeks, make up for it and do several in a week. Of the hundreds of teens with whom we have worked, those teens that develop a realistic and flexible plan are typically the most successful at keeping their anxiety small and manageable and preventing a lapse or relapse. Take some time now to write down the ideas you plan to use in the "Tips to keep anxiety small and manageable" box in My Wellness Plan at the end of this chapter.

KNOW WHO TO ASK FOR SUPPORT. The final piece to include in your Wellness Plan is a list of support people and how to contact them. When something has stirred up your anxious mind, remembering who has helped in the past and how to reach them can be difficult. People who understand what happens to you when you are anxious and what has helped you in the past can help make an anxious episode, well, a little less anxious. Take a moment to think about who has helped you calm your anxious mind. You might include your parents or psychotherapist on your list or the names of your most patient and closest friends. You might include the number of a crisis hotline in your area or the school counselor.

I'm starting college in a few months. I think I can manage my anxiety by using relaxation and problem solving tools and by facing my fears. But I know it's going to be hard and my anxiety might spike because I'll have classes and basketball, and I might pledge a frat. I plan to do 20-minute check-ins on Sunday nights and use my favorite tools during the first few months of college.

—Clay, age 17

MY WELLNESS PLAN

Now it is time to combine everything from this book into a final Wellness Plan. You might go over your Wellness Plan with a parent or even your counselor or psychotherapist. If you begin to feel anxious or worried in the future, it really helps if those who want to help you know just how to do it. Your Wellness Plan lays it all out for them. Although it may be tempting to toss this Wellness Plan into your desk drawer or stuff it in a book, we encourage you to keep your Wellness Plan in a place where you can find it when you need it. You might even consider telling your support people where you keep your plan so that they can find it if you want help.

HAVING FEWER ANXIOUS DAYS AHEAD

Have you ever had an idea or made plans to do something only to hear someone tell you that it will not work or you cannot do it?

Your anxious mind is like that person. It whispers in your ear, predicting that you will fail or scaring you into not trying at all. If you take one thing away from this book, we hope it is that you can learn to listen less to your anxious mind. Although your anxious mind may continue to take up some space in your life, you can rent it less space. The tools in this book, as well as other resources you might try, will help. Remember, from time to time, we all rent space to our anxious minds. Doctors, engineers, professional athletes, and adults from every walk of life, have anxious minds and still lead full and successful lives. An anxious mind does not mean you cannot succeed. An anxious mind does not mean that you cannot be happy. You can have those things and more, even when your anxious mind bugs you from time to time. Good luck!

My Wellness Plan

My accomplishments	
New situations, opportunities, and activities I'd like to try	
Situations that might launch a lapse or relapse	
Important things to remember	
Tips to keep my anxiety small and manageable	
Support people who can help me	

My Favorite Tools

Circle the tools you think will help the most.

Calm Mind Tools

Evidence For and Against	Responsibility Pizza
Time Machine	Confidence Booster

Calm Body Tools

Abdominal breathing	Progressive muscle relaxation
Visualization	Nutrition
Exercise	Sleep

Facing My Fears Tools

Staying Afloat Talk	Jump Back
Distraction	Fear Ladder

Stress-Busting Tools

ICAAN	Negotiation
DEAL	Identifying my feelings

ADDITIONAL RESOURCES

ADDITIONAL FACING MY FEAR PLANS

Bobbie's Facing My Fear Plan

Today's date: June 2

The fear I face today is: Raising my hand to share something during math class.

My anxious track: Everyone will laugh at me or think I'm a show-off.

Think Smart Checklist

CALM MIND TOOL	REMIXED TRACK
Confidence Booster	Even if the other kids do laugh at me or think I'm a show-off, I can handle that because I know that I'm not. My friends know I'm not a show-off and that I'm an okay guy. I'd like the other kids to like me, but if they don't, I can handle that. All I want is a few more friends, not all the kids in my class.

My remixed track: Just because I share something in class doesn't mean that the other kids will think I'm showing off. If I share something and it's wrong, the teacher won't laugh at me because she knows I'm shy, and I'm working on it. I don't think the other kids would laugh, but if they did, my teacher would quiet them down really fast and tell them to knock it off.

(continued)

Bobbie's Facing My Fear Plan *(continued)*

Fear Ladder

SITUATION AND STEP	FEAR RATING (0–10)
Raise my hand in class to give the teacher my opinions.	9
Raise my hand in class and answer a question.	8
Raise my hand in class and ask a question.	6
Raise my hand and agree with another kid's question when I had the same question.	5
Answer a question with the rest of the class.	4
Nod my head to show my teacher I agree with another kid's answer.	3
Write my question in my notebook and asking my teacher the question after class.	2

Bobbie's Fear Thermometer

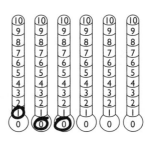

Min's Facing My Fear Plan

Today's date: October 12

The fear I face today is: Touching the kitchen counter with my hands then rubbing my face with my hands and not washing.

My anxious track: The germs on my face will give me a disease, and I'll get really sick.

Think Smart Checklist

CALM MIND TOOL	REMIXED TRACK
Confidence Booster	I can handle feeling dirty and feeling scared. I believe my anxiety is going to go down, the way it has in the past. So I'll just hang out with my fear until it goes away, and it will because it has before. I can handle this.

My remixed track: Touching a dirty kitchen counter isn't dangerous. There's a zero chance I'm going to get sick or catch some disease and die. This is all just my OCD talking and nothing else.

Fear Ladder

SITUATION AND STEP	FEAR RATING (0–10)
Touch the kitchen counter, rub my face with my hands, and not wash my face and hands for 60 minutes.	10
Touch the kitchen counter and not wash my hands for 60 minutes.	9
Touch the kitchen counter, rub my face with my hands, and not wash my face and hands for 45 minutes.	8
Touch the kitchen counter and not wash my hands for 45 minutes.	6

(continued)

Min's Facing My Fear Plan *(continued)*

SITUATION AND STEP	FEAR RATING (0–10)
Touch the kitchen counter, rub my face with my hands, and not wash my face and hands for 30 minutes.	5
Touch the kitchen counter and not wash my hands for 30 minutes.	4
Touch the kitchen counter, rub my face with my hands, and not wash my face and hands for 15 minutes.	3
Touch the kitchen counter and not wash my hands for 15 minutes.	2

Min's Fear Thermometer

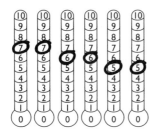

READINGS FOR TEENS

Fiction

Buffie, M. (1998). *Angels turn their backs*. New York: Kids Can Press.
Harrar, G. (2004). *Not as crazy as I seem*. New York: Graphia.
Hesser, T. S. (1998). *Kissing doorknobs*. New York: Delacorte Press.
Tashjian, J. (1999). *Multiple choice*. New York: Henry Holt.

Non-fiction

Fox, A., & Kirschner, R. (2005). *Too stressed to think? A teen guide to staying sane when life makes you crazy*. Minneapolis, MN: Free Spirit.
Hipp, E. (2008). *Fighting invisible tigers: Stress management for teens* (3rd ed.). Minneapolis, MN: Free Spirit.
Kant, J. D., Franklin, M., & Andrews, L. W. (2008). *The thought that counts: A firsthand account of one teenager's experience with obsessive–compulsive disorder*. New York: Oxford University Press.

READINGS FOR PARENTS

Anxiety

Dacey, J. S., & Fiore, L. B. (2000). *Your anxious child: How parents and teachers can relieve anxiety in children*. San Francisco: Jossey-Bass.
Foa, E. B., & Andrews, L. W. (2006). *If your adolescent has an anxiety disorder: An essential resource for parents*. New York: Oxford University Press.
Monahon, C. (1993). *Children and trauma: A guide for parents and professionals*. San Francisco: Jossey-Bass.
Rapee, R. M., Wignall, A., Spence, S. H., Cobham, V., & Lyneham, H. (2008). *Helping your anxious child: A step-by-step guide for parents* (2nd ed.). Oakland, CA: New Harbinger.
Spencer, E. D., DuPont, R. L., & DuPont, C. M. (2003). *The anxiety cure for kids: A guide for parents*. Hoboken, NJ: John Wiley & Sons.
Wagner, A. P. (2005). *Worried no more: Help and hope for anxious children* (2nd ed.). Rochester, NY: Lighthouse Press.

Obsessive–Compulsive Disorder

Chansky, T. E. (2000). *Freeing your child from obsessive–compulsive disorder: A powerful, practical program for parents of children and adolescents.* New York: Crown.

Fitzgibbons, L., & Pedrick, C. (2003). *Helping your child with OCD: A workbook for parents of children with obsessive–compulsive disorder.* Oakland, CA: New Harbinger.

Wagner, A. P. (2002). *What to do when your child has obsessive–compulsive disorder: Strategies and solutions.* Rochester, NY: Lighthouse Press.

Waltz, M. (2000). *Obsessive–compulsive disorder: Help for children and adolescents.* Sebastopol, CA: O'Reilly.

Medication

Elliott, G. R. (2006). *Medicating young minds: How to know if psychiatric drugs will help or hurt your child.* New York: Stewart, Tabori & Chang.

Wilens, T. E. (2008). *Straight talk about psychiatric medications for kids* (3rd ed.). New York: Guilford.

ONLINE RESOURCES

Professional Associations

The following professional associations provide teens and parents with or brochures, tips, and articles on the psychological and emotional issues that affect a person's physical and emotional well-being, as well as information about referrals and how to locate a therapist.

- Academy of Cognitive Therapy
  www.academyofct.org
- American Academy of Child and Adolescent Psychiatry
  www.aacap.org

- American Psychiatric Association
  www.psych.org, www.healthyminds.org
- American Psychological Association
  www.apa.org, www.apahelpcenter.org, http://locator.apa.org
- Association for Behavioral and Cognitive Therapies
  www.abct.org

Specific Disorders

Below are a few organizations that are dedicated to informing and education the public, health care professionals, and media about specific anxiety or anxiety-related disorders. They provide teens and parents with information on the specific disorder, coping with it, locating support groups, and more.

- Anxiety Disorders Association of America
  www.adaa.org, www.gotanxiety.org
- Obsessive–Compulsive Foundation, Inc.
  www.ocfoundation.org
- Trichotillomania Learning Center
  www.trich.org

Health Information

The U.S. Department of Health and Human Services and provides parents and teens a wealth of information on physical and mental health.

- Food and Drug Administration
  www.fda.gov
- National Institute of Mental Health (NIMH)
  www.nimh.nih.gov
- National Institutes of Health (NIH)
  www.nih.gov

BIBLIOGRAPHY

Chapter 1

Foa E. B., & Andrews, L. W. (2006). *If your adolescent has an anxiety disorder: An essential resource for parents.* New York: Oxford University Press.

Chapter 7

Blumenthal, J. A., Sherwood, A., Gullette, E. C. D., Georgiades, A., & Tweedy, D. (2002). Biobehavioral approaches to the treatment of essential hypertension. *Journal of Consulting and Clinical Psychology, 70(3)*, 569–589.

Gillham, J. E., Brunwasser, S. M., & Freres, D. R. (2007). Preventing depression in early adolescence: The Penn Resiliency Program. In J. R. Z. Abela & B. L. Hankin (Eds.), *Handbook of depression in children and adolescents* (pp. 309–332). New York: Guilford.

Chapter 8

American Academy of Pediatrics. (2003). *Caring for your teenager: The complete and authoritative guide.* (D. E. Greydanus & P. Bashe, Eds.). New York: Bantam.

American Academy of Pediatrics Committee on Nutrition. (2009). *Pediatric nutrition handbook* (6th ed.). (R. E. Kleinman, Ed.). Elk Grove Village, IL: American Academy of Pediatrics.

Bourne, E. J. (2005). *The anxiety & phobia workbook* (4th ed.). Oakland, CA: New Harbinger.

Carskadon, M. A. (Ed.). (2002). *Adolescent sleep patterns: Biological, social, and psychological influences.* New York: Cambridge University Press.

National Sleep Foundation. (2006). *National Sleep Foundation 2006 Sleep in America Poll Highlights and Key Findings.* Retrieved from http://www.sleepfoundation.org/atf/cf/{F6BF2668-A1B4-4FE8-8D1A-A5D39340D9CB}/Highlights_facts_06.pdf

National Sleep Foundation. (2006). *Summary of findings of the 2006 Sleep in America poll.*Retrieved from http://www.sleepfoundation.org/atf/cf/{F6BF2668-A1B4-4FE8-8D1A-A5D39340D9CB}/2006_summary_of_findings.pdf

U.S. Food and Drug Administration Center for Food Safety and Applied Nutrition. (2004). *How to Understand and Use the Nutrition Facts Label.* Retrieved from http://www.cfsan.fda.gov/~dms/foodlab.html

Wilson, R. (2009). *Don't panic: Taking control of anxiety attacks* (3rd ed.). New York: Harper Collins.

Chapter 9

Walkup, J. T., Albano, A. M., Piacentini, J., Birmaher, B., Compton, S. N., Sherrill, J. T., et al. (2008). Cognitive behavioral therapy, sertraline, or a combination in childhood anxiety. *New England Journal of Medicine, 359(26),* 2753–2766.

ACKNOWLEDGEMENTS

A great many people have supported the writing of this book. We are particularly grateful to several experienced clinicians who took time from their busy schedules to review parts of this book and offer their thoughtful suggestions. We thank: Brad Berman, Glen Elliott, Jerry Hester, Mary Jones, and Anya Ho. We thank Joan Davidson, Janie Hong, Jackie Persons, and Dan Weiner, our colleagues at the San Francisco Bay Area Center for Cognitive Therapy who are the calming and supportive harbor that we call our professional home.

We thank Becky Shaw, editor at Magination Press, for taking on this book project and encouraging us early on. We extend a special thank you to Kristine Enderle, managing editor at Magination Press, for her patience, support, and great ideas that improved the book on many levels. In addition, we thank those members of the Advisory Board of Magination Press and the American Psychological Association who reviewed early drafts. Their thoughtful guidance and suggestions improved the accuracy and overall content of the book.

We thank our families, Luann, Madeline, Olivia, Adam and Jack, for their forbearance with our many weekends away from home. We truly could not have done this without you.

But in particular, we are grateful to the many anxious teens and their parents who have come to us for help over the years. Much of the courage and perseverance that we needed to finish this book, we learned from you. Thank you.

ABOUT THE AUTHORS

Michael A. Tompkins, PhD, is a licensed psychologist and a founding partner of the San Francisco Bay Area Center for Cognitive Therapy; Assistant Clinical Professor at the University of California, Berkeley; and a Founding Fellow of the Academy of Cognitive Therapy. He specializes in cognitive–behavior therapy for anxiety and mood disorders in adults, adolescents, and children. Dr. Tompkins is the author or co-author of numerous articles and chapters on cognitive–behavior therapy and related topics, including the book, *Using Homework in Psychotherapy: Strategies, Guidelines, and Forms,* and an American Psychological Association book and videotape series (with Jacqueline B. Persons and Joan Davidson) *Essential Components of Cognitive–Behavior Therapy for Depression.* Currently, he is at work on a book titled, *Cognitive–Behavior Therapy for Obsessive–Compulsive Disorder in Youth: A Step-by-Step Guide* to be published by the American Psychological Association. He lives in Oakland, California with his wife and two daughters.

Katherine A. Martinez, PsyD, is a licensed psychologist and partner at the San Francisco Bay Area Center for Cognitive Therapy. She specializes in cognitive–behavioral assessment and treatment for children and adolescents with anxiety, mood, and attention deficit disorders. Dr. Martinez provides parent effectiveness training to parents and caregivers, and conducts workshops and trainings on cognitive-behavior therapy for youth at the University of California, Berkeley Extension and Children's Hospital and Research Center of Oakland. She lives in Oakland, California with her husband and son.

ABOUT THE ILLUSTRATOR

Michael Sloan spent several years working as a printmaker in Europe before moving to New York City. His illustrations first appeared on the Op-Ed page of *The New York Times,* where he remains a frequent contributor to the Letters column. He has created illustrations for many clients including *Fortune, The Village Voice, The New Yorker,* Barnes & Noble, and *The San Francisco Chronicle.* Michael is also the author of the Professor Nimbus books and comics. His second graphic novel, *The Heresy of Professor Nimbus,* was awarded a silver medal in the sequential category of the Society of Illustrators 49th Annual Exhibition.

ABOUT MAGINATION PRESS

Magination Press publishes self-help books for kids and the adults in their lives. We are an imprint of the American Psychological Association, the largest scientific and professional organization representing psychologists in the United States and the largest association of psychologists worldwide.